READ MY CLIPS

Lewis Grossberger

READ MY CLIPS

Media Person Cuts Up

Random House

New York

Portions of this work were originally published in different form in *Gentlemen's Quarterly, Rolling Stone, 7 Days,* and *Vanity Fair.*

Grateful acknowledgment is made to Straight Arrow Publishers, Inc. for permission to reprint "Triumph of the Wheel" by Lewis Grossberger from the December 4, 1986, issue of *Rolling Stone* Magazine. Copyright © 1986 by Straight Arrow Publishers. All rights reserved. Reprinted by permission.

Library of Congress Cataloging-in-Publication Data
Grossberger, Lewis.
Read my clips : media person cuts up / by Lewis Grossberger.
p.   cm.
ISBN 0-679-73414-7
1. Journalists—Humor. 2. American wit and humor. I. Title.
PN6231.J68G76 1991   818'.5402—dc20   90-52888

Manufactured in the United States of America
Book design by J. K. Lambert
2 4 6 8 9 7 5 3
First Edition

Much of the material in this book originally appeared in *7 Days* magazine, although often in a different, slightly less coherent form. "Triumph of the Wheel" was first published in *Rolling Stone*, "The Mad Monk and His Screaming Heads" in *GQ*, and "To Sleep, Perchance to Scream" in *Vanity Fair*, though all have been enhanced through the miracle of rewrite.

To my mother

Facing the press is more difficult than bathing a leper.

MOTHER TERESA

Acknowledgments

The author sincerely wishes to thank everyone who
ever helped him in any way and also those who were
not in a position to help but would have
had they been able.

Contents

READ MY CLIPS

Pleased to Media

Many years ago, E. M. Forster wrote a science-fiction story titled "The Machine Stops." It told of a future society in which people sat in little cubicles all day communicating with electronic devices. All needs were met by machinery. Everyone stayed in their compartments and eventually they couldn't leave even if they wanted to because their legs had withered from disuse.*

We're getting there.

Already it's possible to stay home all day, have food and other essentials delivered, perform all necessary tasks via computer, fax, telephone, and electric can opener, and never go outside.

You have just read a frighteningly accurate description of the life of Media Person.

It's possible you may not have heard of Media Person as he has never been on the Oprah Winfrey show. He is the man who gave

---

*After a while the machinery broke down, and being totally helpless, the entire populace died a horrible death, which is perhaps why "The Machine Stops" has never been made into a major motion picture.

up real life because it was interfering with his compulsive need to read newspapers and magazines and watch television (usually at the same time). That is now all he does.

Media Person is a kind of throwback but also a throw-ahead. He's an urban hermit. Unlike old-fashioned hermits who used to live in the woods, shun all human contact, and eventually begin having fascinating conversations with turnips, Media Person stays in touch.

Because he constantly monitors the media, Media Person is better connected to the world than most of the people who are out running around in it every day, exhausting themselves and exposing themselves to potentially lethal hazards such as electrocution by stepping on a manhole cover, which in 1989 killed an unsuspecting dog in New York City as its owner took it for an evening walk.

But it is not just news that Media Person craves. As a well-rounded human being (the diet hasn't been working lately), he also needs entertainment. Media Person watches movies, sports, spectacles, parades, cartoons, and commercials. He reads advice columnists, horoscopes, theater reviews, and want ads. He does crosswords and acrostics. He watches *National Geographic* documentaries on the life cycle of the African baobab tree. He watches Geraldo Rivera discuss the sex habits of the African baobab tree with a panel of bark molesters. He delves deep into Mount Media, the mystical, snow-capped pile of magazines growing ever higher on his living-room floor.

Media Person's whole life is media.

This is why he is uniquely qualified to help you learn how to keep the media from driving you crazy. Perhaps you've noticed how hard they've been trying.

Don't blame them. They can't help themselves. First, there's too much media, too much information in the world. No one is sure exactly when it happened, but at some point in the '6os or early '7os, "the news" turned into "the media" and began going out of control. Once news had been a helpful source of information on the world around us. Now it became a jumbled, confusing mass of scary, dangerous noise.

Also it seemed to be signaling that the world around us had gone hopelessly berserk and become a menace to our health. Was this really true or was it just media hysteria?

Both, actually. One reason there's more media in our lives is that outside gets more and more dangerous so people stay inside and watch TV. As hazardous as media can be, it is less so than reality, which Media Person avoids as much as possible.

A lot of media-battered people have tried to kick the habit but few could last long. Giving up alcohol, drugs, or cigarettes is easy compared to giving up media.

Media Person took the opposite course. He jumped in whole hog. Total immersion. Yes, he was risking his mental health, not to mention his eyesight, but it was worth it.

Because by doing so, he was able to develop the proper technique for dealing with modern media. Reduced to its simplest terms, that technique consists of three basic steps: 1. Observation. 2. Intense ridicule. 3. Derisive laughter.

This, Media Person believes, is the only effective defense against the media juggernaut, which every day hurls at us massive amounts of news, entertainment, advertising, infotainment, docudrama, adverteasing, infoganda, and whatever new junk they've come up with this week.

Read this book and soon, as if by magic, you will have absorbed Media Person's attitude. You will then be mediaproof, and you can turn on the news without fear.

Not that Media Person wants to overdramatize or anything but, frankly, it's your only chance to survive into the twenty-first century.

A Better Caliber of Behavior

One of the many reasons Media Person stays home is to avoid facing the uncharted complexities of modern etiquette in our rapidly changing society.

In New York, where Media Person lives, virtually all social interactions now end in gunplay. This raises complex questions of correct behavior.

Two recent examples from the newspapers:

At a bas mitzvah held in the Flatbush section of Brooklyn, a guest was shot dead after an argument broke out over music selection.

In a Bronx theater showing *Batman* two patrons began blasting away (with results fatal to one) after disagreeing over who was first in the popcorn line.

Both affairs involved an ever more common social situation: An individual feels affronted and announces with some emotion that he is going off to get his gun.

The interesting etiquette question here is how the other involved party should respond. By all means, one wishes to do the polite thing, but what is it?

One's first instinct might be to run away, thus potentially saving one or more lives, a quantity of ammunition, and much wear and tear on police and medical personnel.

But wouldn't that be an insult to the aggrieved individual and also the height of rudeness?

Remember, this person has gone out of his way to inform you that he intends to return with his gun. In effect, he has made an appointment. One should always try to keep an appointment.

In both of the above cases, the second person did in fact decide that appropriate conduct was to wait patiently on the premises while the affronted party procured his gun and returned. Firing ensued.

This certainly contradicts the popular view of New Yorkers as rude and insensitive to the needs of others.

However, it also indicates that a large amount of ammunition is flying around out there and that Media Person will be remaining at home behind triply locked doors for the foreseeable future.

The Laws
of the Media

The Laws of the Media, inscribed on two stone tablets, were given down to humankind in June 1974, by a gigantic hand that crashed through the ceiling of the television studio where Walter Cronkite, at that time the Voice of the Lord,* was broadcasting *The CBS Evening News*. Without missing a beat, the unflappable superanchor read the tablets, incorporating the new material into his program so smoothly that most viewers hardly realized anything untoward had occurred—though a woman in Pompton Lakes, New Jersey, reportedly fell victim to an irresistible compulsion to make a calf of gold and drag it in front of her TV set.

- YOU SHALL NEVER TAKE THE TOP NEWSPAPER ON THE PILE.
- IF NO TELEVISION CAMERA IS THERE TO RECORD IT, IT DIDN'T REALLY HAPPEN.
- A NEWSPAPER COLUMNIST'S PHOTOGRAPH SHALL BE AT LEAST TEN YEARS OLD.

*An office later passed to Ted Koppel.

- THERE SHALL NEVER BE A FUNNY MADE-FOR-TV MOVIE.
- IT TAKES THREE OF ANYTHING TO MAKE A TREND.
- THE FRIEND YOU'VE LONG URGED TO TRY YOUR FAVORITE TV SHOW SHALL WATCH ON THE DAY THE WEAKEST EPISODE OF THE SEASON IS SHOWN.
- *THE WALL STREET JOURNAL* SHALL CONTAIN ONLY ONE INTERESTING ARTICLE A DAY.
- SOME PEOPLE SHALL SET THE CLOCK ON THEIR VCRS, SOME SHALL TAPE A SHOW WHILE OUT OF THE HOUSE, AND SOME SHALL TAPE ONE SHOW WHILE WATCHING ANOTHER, BUT NO ONE ON EARTH SHALL KNOW HOW TO DO ALL THREE.
- YOU SHALL NOT ABOMINATE DEATH, FOR WITHOUT IT THERE COULD BE NO NEWSPAPERS.
- ANY CALLER TO A RADIO TALK SHOW SHALL BEGIN BY ANNOUNCING HOW LONG HE'S BEEN LISTENING TO THE SHOW AND WHETHER OR NOT HE'S CALLED BEFORE, EVEN THOUGH NO ONE ELSE CARES.
- EVERY TIME HE REVIEWS A FARCE, A THEATER CRITIC SHALL DIGRESS FOR AN EXTENSIVE LECTURE ON THE IMPORTANCE TO THE GENRE OF DOORS AND THEIR SLAMMING.
- ANY MAIL YOU RECEIVE MARKED "IMPORTANT DOCUMENTS ENCLOSED—OPEN IMMEDIATELY" SHALL BE THROWN OUT UNOPENED AS THERE IS NOTHING INSIDE OF THE SLIGHTEST INTEREST.
- THERE SHALL BE A VAST MULTITUDE OF MAGAZINES IN THE LAND YET NONE SHALL BE WORTH A DAMN.
- HE WHOM THE MEDIA CREATES, THE MEDIA SHALL DESTROY, BUT OL' MAN REAGAN HE JUST KEEPS ROLLIN' ALONG.
- IN ANY OF THE HOMES OF THE PEOPLE SHALL BE FOUND BETWEEN EIGHT AND TWELVE TELEVISION SCHEDULES BUT NOWHERE IS IT DISCLOSED WHAT IS ON THE RADIO.
- A MINISERIES BASED UPON A BOOK OF HERMAN WOUK SHALL BE THREE TIMES LONGER THAN LIFE ITSELF.
- A PUBLIC FIGURE WHO TRANSGRESSES WICKEDLY SHALL BE CAST INTO MEDIA HELL TO BE PLAGUED FOR ETERNITY BY THE STINGS OF HEADLINES AND THE JESTS OF LATE-NIGHT

COMEDIANS. BUT IF HE SHALL GO TO A TALK SHOW AND
HUMBLE HIMSELF BEFORE THE PEOPLE AND WEEP AND APOL-
OGIZE, THEN SHALL HE RETURN TO A STATE OF GRACE.

- ITS SPEED SHALL RANGE FROM 10 TO 45 MILES PER SECOND
  AND WHEN NEARING THE EARTH, IT SHALL BECOME HEATED
  TO INCANDESCENCE BY FRICTION.*

- A RISING STAR SHALL BE PUFFED, A BLAZING STAR PILLORIED,
  A FADING STAR FORGOTTEN.†

*Actually, that's a Law of the Meteor. Sorry but this chapter came up a bit
short, so Media Person used the closest thing he could find to fill.

†See, now that *sounds* like a Law of the Meteor, but it's really a Law of the
Media. This stuff can get tricky.

It Walks! It Talks! It Puts On a Sweater!

Some people complain about the superficiality of television news, but in fact the networks have made great strides in the past few years. Even with reduced budgets and staffs, network news executives have been able to introduce important innovations.

Perhaps the most impressive of these was the discovery that anchors could move. Previously anchors never left the anchor desk and many were actually chained to it to ensure that they would not inadvertently go to lunch in the middle of the newscast.

Moving the anchor demonstrated to skeptical critics that an anchor can do much more than just sit in a studio in New York and read copy written by someone else. He can also stand in front of the Kremlin and read copy written by someone else.

Today, all network anchors keep a suitcase under the anchor desk. At the first sign of crisis, they dash to the airport, followed by camera crew and hairdresser. Within hours, they are broadcasting live from the big event, often not even needing to pause and observe it.

When it comes to moving, few anchors can match the talented

Tom Brokaw of NBC. This is a man who understands motion in all its facets. Take *down*, for instance.

Reading a *New York Times* article by Bill Keller on the terrible Armenian earthquake of 1989, Media Person came across this remarkable scene:

> A chartered helicopter descended into the gruesome remains of Spitak. Zombie-like survivors gaped up from their grief to see a neatly coiffed man, clad in a white turtleneck and natty blue anorak, take up a position before the colossal ruin of the Spitak bread factory. It was Tom Brokaw of the NBC *Nightly News*, a star in the heart of darkness.

Only one day after swooping Zeus-style into the Armenian rubble, the versatile Brokaw rushed to Geneva to cover an important United Nations speech by Yasir Arafat. He had demolished his rivals, the sluggish Dan Rather and the torpid Peter Jennings, who sat motionless back on the dull North American continent, reading their tedious copy in stodgy studios with no excuse for donning a natty anorak.

When rebellion broke out in China, the bold executives of NBC were ready to go still further. Brokaw would not merely stand in Tienanmen Square like the others. He would become the first *bicycling* anchorman.

There he was, pedaling through Peking or Beijing or whatever they're calling it now, both bicycling *and talking*. It was an extraordinary technological feat, accomplished apparently by mounting a camera on another bicycle that kept pace with Brokaw's mouth. Television history had been made and transportation history as well.

Media Person realized that the achievement could lead to even bigger developments. Why, next a network could attach permanent wheels and a motor to the anchor desk. Freed from the confines of the studio, packs of exuberant anchors would roar out of their stations and range across the land, nattering as they went.

Over at ABC, Roone Arledge could put his stars Sam Donaldson and Diane Sawyer on a motorbike built for two.

Eventually we would see evolving a whole new breed of highly mobile TV newspeople—tap-dancing anchors, skating anchors, skiing anchors, maybe even parachuting anchors. Someday, perhaps, a Tom Brokaw could be loaded into a ballistic missile and rocketed within minutes to an ongoing event, be it riot, hurricane, or assassination.

It wasn't long before CBS had an answer to Brokaw's bicycle act. The step was so simple yet so elegant that, looking back, it was hard to believe no one had ever thought of it before.

Dan Rather stood up.

Just like that. There he was on *The CBS Evening News*, standing and delivering. It was inspired. And Dan Rather was the perfect man to attempt it. Rather had already made history by being the first anchor to wear a sweater on camera. He had carried that off with an aplomb and sangfroid that few others could have matched. Even the great Cronkite had never attempted it.

Of course CBS knew it was taking a great risk. Aggressive, high-strung, more than a little eccentric, Dan Rather was a good, serious reporter who, in a sane world (i.e., one without network television) probably would have ended up managing editor of a small newspaper or chief of detectives in Dallas, Texas. Unfortunately he became an actor (actor, anchor—same thing), a job for which he was ill-suited. Try as he might to achieve folksy, regular-Joe affability, Rather could never disguise his peculiar intensity. It made the mass audience nervous. Made *himself* nervous, too. As an anchor, Rather's instincts were out of whack. All the wrong hormones were always flooding the wrong glands, and he was constantly getting into bizarre scrapes and imbroglios that made him look bad in the press.

Thus it was that his first attempt to read the news standing up ended in disaster. Rather stood up, all right. But he didn't leave it at that. He began to walk. He walked off camera and right out of the studio, causing the entire CBS network to go black for seven minutes. In his love of the dramatic, Rather had gone too far.*

---

*The network put out a story that Rather had been angered by a tennis broadcast running overtime, which was generally believed.

Despite the fiasco, CBS decided on another attempt. This time, after much coaching and rehearsal, Rather succeeded. Media Person was watching that night and when he realized that Rather was actually upright and reading, he gasped.

Of course, Media Person knew that the other networks would not take standing up lying down.

There would be moves and countermoves. Perhaps Jennings would read the news standing on his head. And Brokaw, that wily competitor, might be forced to take to the trapeze. There were rumors that CNN's anchors were in a gym secretly forming a human pyramid.

But all that was in the future. For the moment, Media Person could only salute Dan Rather's courage and skill with a personal *hommage*. He got up on his own two feet and began watching the news in this difficult new position. Yes. It seemed right. As long as Dan Rather stood, so would Media Person. It was the least he could do.

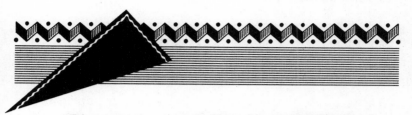

Gimme That Old Tabloid Religion (Or, Billy Martin's Up There Playing Ball with God)

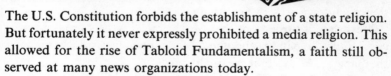

The U.S. Constitution forbids the establishment of a state religion. But fortunately it never expressly prohibited a media religion. This allowed for the rise of Tabloid Fundamentalism, a faith still observed at many news organizations today.

It is a quirky creed that makes little sense to outsiders but is comforting to the devout, who practice its few simple rituals compulsively. Most often found working for raucous, sensational, big-city newspapers,* but also numerous in TV news, Tabloid Fundamentalists have two main concerns:

*Some people today think *tabloid* refers to supermarket rags like the *National Enquirer*. Technically, the word denotes only size: any newspaper half as big as a standard broadsheet paper. But of course tabloid is also a state of mind that can be found at many publications as well as broadcast-news organizations. It's the difference between "Local Woman Dies in Domestic Mishap" and "Terror Tot Slays Napping Mom with Electric Carving Knife."

1. Any time a plane crash or other serious accident occurs, they must find evidence of a miracle therein.
2. When celebrities expire, they must determine if the deceased is bound for heaven or hell.

The first is the more important. Miracles are the cornerstone of the faith and a devout Tabloid Fundamentalist proclaims them whenever possible. Usually headlines are the medium of choice.

In a strange 1989 case, one of those two-day media sensations that blight our era, a small plane splashed into the Atlantic and the occupant, Thomas Root, who apparently had been flying unconscious for quite some time, was found alive. The Tabloid Fundamentalists immediately agreed that God had personally intervened, although a small theological dispute arose over what form the deity took.

The *New York Post* announced that

GOD WAS HIS CO-PILOT

But *New York Newsday* insisted that

GOD WAS HIS AUTOPILOT

Neither paper criticized God's landing technique, even though the touchdown was rather rough.

Next day, it turned out that Mr. Miracle had acquired a suspicious bullet hole in his abdomen. Media Person anxiously scanned the papers, fearing that he might read:

POLICE PICK UP GOD FOR QUESTIONING

It didn't happen, although ABC did pick up Thomas Root and put him on its magazine show *Prime Time Live*. Media Person made sure to watch and was rewarded by hearing Diane Sawyer proclaim Root's survival a miracle.

The Tabloid Fundamentalist takes a starkly pessimistic view of airplane malfunctions. His religion teaches that whenever an airplane gets in trouble, everyone aboard must die. If they don't, the only possible explanation is the miraculous.

Say a plane carrying 189 passengers has a jammed landing gear and makes an emergency landing at an airport in North Carolina. The landing is shaky but no one is killed or seriously injured. Now how to explain this? Could it be a matter of effective aircraft design plus elementary principles of aerodynamics? A cool and competent pilot? Good presence of mind on the part of air controllers? No. The Tabloid Fundamentalist rejects all rational possibilities.

"It was a miracle," all the TV anchors and tabloid headlines will say.

Something that's hard for Media Person to understand is why the Almighty is given credit for snatching victims from death but never the blame for causing their problems in the first place. But Tabloid Fundamentalists are mysteriously selective. Maybe it's Satan causing all the trouble, but if so, why do the media withhold this information?

In another typical tabloid miracle, an unfortunate boy from Queens, New York, fell on a fence spike, which penetrated his skull, though not fatally. The *New York Daily News* bannered:

MR. LUCKY

This gave a whole new meaning to the word *lucky*. Could Media Person be thought cynical for feeling that a more fitting recipient could have been found for the title "Mr. Lucky"? Say, for instance, any of the five or six billion earthlings who *didn't* have a spike impale his head that day?

Of course, creative Tabloid Fundamentalists can find the hand of God not only in disasters but in almost any process whose inner workings they don't fully comprehend. When the sports tabloid *The National* began publishing, columnist Dave Kindred attempted to explain its newfangled production system, which he said involved "electronic whizzes" beaming signals to an orbiting satellite.

"What is this, dear reader," he asked, "if not a miracle?"

Science would be Media Person's guess, but anyone responding thus would face the threat of excommunication by the Tabloid Fundamentalists.

The other important function of Tabloid Fundamentalism is ferreting out where newly deceased people, particularly celebrities, will be spending their afterlife. Exactly how Tabloid Fundamentalists uncover this information Media Person has no idea. Maybe the wire services have managed to open bureaus on the scene. Maybe there is public relations after death. But somehow, they know.

When Sammy Davis, Jr., died, the *Globe*, a sleazy supermarket paper, bannered

HE'LL BE A STAR

IN HEAVEN, TOO

After some briefly notorious but now forgotten psychopathic criminal became suddenly defunct, the *New York Post* headlined:

KILLER TOOK HIS SECRET TO HELL

Media Person avidly read the story in the futile hope that a *Post* correspondent was in attendance and would provide firsthand accounts of sulfur and brimstone along with quotes from the deceased on his new accommodations.

But the most popular medium for celebrity-afterlife spotting is the editorial cartoon. Whenever consensus bad guys expire, the cartoonists unhesitatingly send them straight to hell. After Ayatollah Khomeini died, Media Person counted three editorial cartoons portraying his arrival among the damned, and on the *Tonight* show, Jay Leno did it verbally. "The ayatollah was buried face down," he said. "That's so he could see where he was going."

Any famous person who is not a known serial murderer or a certified Enemy of America is likely to be reported en route to paradise. Upon dying, Billy Martin, the noted alcoholic, brawler, and recidivist New York Yankees manager, was appointed a legend and shipped heavenward by the New York tabloids. The *Post* prominently quoted a Yankee fan as saying that Billy was now "playing ball with God." It was unfortunate that no box score was furnished as Media Person has often wondered what position the Big Guy plays up there.

But it wasn't easy for Martin to get to the celestial game, according to Gary Markstein, cartoonist for the Tribune Papers of Arizona. He portrayed the truculent Yankee kicking dirt on an exasperated St. Peter, who finally says, "All right, all right, I'll let you in."

Such confrontations or mixups at the pearly gates are a frequent occurrence in editorial cartoons. The *New York Post*'s Bay Rigby drew Malcolm Forbes, the late billionaire magazine publisher, arriving on his much-publicized motorcycle only to be greeted by a confused gatekeeper, who checks the ledger and says, "Forbes . . . Malcolm . . . I thought you were a Hell's Angel." The same paper headlined its account of the Forbes funeral:

HARLEY HEAVEN
FORBES RIDES OFF INTO A VERY GOLDEN SUNSET

When the designer Halston died, Rigby found him in heaven helping a bearded fellow into a stylish jacket and saying, "Oh, yes, that's you, St. Peter, robes went out years ago."

But Media Person's favorite *Post* afterlife sendoff came in a moving and poignant obituary for a beloved sea lion named Fin, who suffered a fatal plunge into a drained pool at the Central Park Zoo. (Beloved yes, bright, no.) The *Post* reported that a zoo visitor had told her son, "He's gone to sea lion heaven."

Where he's no doubt playing ball with Billy Martin, riding on the back of Malcolm Forbes's Harley, and getting tossed delicious fish from God—that is when God isn't busy plucking people out of crashing planes.

Astounding Facts from Way in Back

Some people think that *The New York Times* is a dull newspaper, but this is erroneous. In fact the *Times* is full of fascinating, gruesome, titillating tidbits that can be as hilarious and strange as anything in the *National Enquirer*.

The misconception arises from long-established editing practices at the *Times*. Due to their overwhelming need to seem important and serious, which they equate with being solemn and dull, the top editors have trained their staff to hide the best stuff way in the back of the paper at the bottom of long, gray columns of impenetrable type where only obsessed fanatics like Media Person ever go.

This is why Media Person recommends that anyone attempting to read the *Times* start at the end and read from the bottom up. Otherwise, long before reaching the interesting material, you will fall asleep.

To illustrate, here are a few gems Media Person has extracted from the slag where until now they lay hidden, safe from prying eyes:

(All AFFWIB are guaranteed gleaned from actual articles in the actual *New York Times*.)

- When they left the White House and moved to a new home in Bel Air, California, Ronald and Nancy Reagan had their street address changed to 668 because the original, 666, is said in the New Testament Book of Revelations to be "the number of the beast," that is, Satan.
- According to a book about the civil war in Rhodesia (now Zimbabwe), some whites torturing a black man kept playing a John Denver record over and over with the volume turned up.
- Student volunteers at Stanford University run a store called Ye Olde Safer Sex Shoppe, which provides condoms to students free or at cost.
- At the economic summit at Williamsburg in 1983, President Reagan confessed to startled aides that he had watched *The Sound of Music* on television instead of reading his briefing books.
- Among the approximately two thousand dead Catholics being investigated by the Vatican for possible elevation to sainthood is Princess Grace of Monaco.
- Half a million mice were wiped out in a laboratory fire in Maine—by far the worst rodent tragedy in U.S. history. "This is a national disaster," said a lab official.
- Deng Xiaoping, China's senior leader, warned other top Chinese officials not to listen to him if he starts to say "crazy things" as he gets older and less clear-minded.
- Thousands of tumbleweeds, some as big as cars, blew into Mobridge, South Dakota, virtually burying the town of 4,180 people. Tractors and front-end loaders removed an estimated thirty tons of the dry prairie weeds.
- Scientists say that methane gas emitted from the intestines of common farm animals is one of the main causes of the greenhouse effect.
- The great composer Franz Schubert, who died of a venereal

disease, may have been a habitual child molester, according to a prominent psychobiographer.

- Major General Gray Allison, Liberia's defense minister, was charged with murdering a policeman and cutting out his heart so that a witch doctor could use it to make "juju" (harsh medicine) against President Samuel K. Doe, whom Allison allegedly sought to overthrow. Allison and his wife, known as devout Christians, had previously been named Liberia's father and mother of the year.

- Generoso Pope, late owner of the *National Enquirer*, used to measure the grass on the office grounds almost every day. He required it to be precisely four inches high.

- Many members of the audience attending Wagner's Ring Cycle at the Metropolitan Opera in New York actually remained awake throughout the entire performance.

- Alexander B. Klots, a leading authority on butterflies, died on the same day as Louis Neumiller, former chairman of Caterpillar, Inc.

- Political experts believe that due to a delay before George Bush's presidential oath-taking, J. Danforth Quayle was acting president of the United States for three and a half minutes.

- The cult leader and guru formerly known as Bhagwan Shree Rajneesh changed his name after discovering that Bhagwan means "genitals" in Sanskrit.

- Ten people were arrested in Massachusetts for illegally killing more than four hundred black bears for their gallbladders. When dried and powdered, the organs are prized as aphrodisiacs in the Orient, bringing more money than cocaine.

- Millions of Africans and Indians suffer from Guinea worm, a parasitic condition in which a worm sometimes *a yard long* crawls out of a blister in the victim's body (usually the legs or feet), taking as long as three weeks to fully emerge. In one case, up to forty worms exited a single victim.

- The Library of Congress' periodical room was closed for four days to allow for eradication of head lice. "We found them in *Barron's, Architectural Digest,* and *The Wall Street Journal*," an exterminator said.

- All letters sent out from the office of Britain's Prince Charles must be checked for errors by the royal heir himself because, in his words, "English is taught so bloody badly."
- Bacteria propel themselves by means of tiny electric motors that rotate their filaments.*

*Media Person doesn't believe this drivel for a second, but there it was in *The New York Times*, so what can he do? Send your protests there, not to MP.

How to Be a
Stellar Quidnunc

Are you stuck in a low-paying, dead-end job that leaves your vast potential untapped?

Well, maybe it's time to consider a career change. Why not take a few moments of your spare time right now and let Media Person show you how to make big bucks and meet glamorous celebrities while enjoying one of America's most lucrative and exciting professions: writing a gossip column.

Gossip columnists want you to believe their success comes from a rare talent for digging up celebrity scuttlebutt. Bunk. Here is the shocking truth: Anyone can do it. The trick is all in the *writing*, and Media Person can teach you to master that simple skill in no time.

Gossip columnists don't really need to be good reporters. In fact, they don't need to report at all. Oh, they can, if they wish, bop off every night to the many parties and social events they get invited to (though not because of their magnetic personalities) and allow publicity-hungry celebrities and celebrity sycophants to suck up to them and slip them items. But it's not really necessary. Those at the top of the gossip pole usually have assistants (called legmen) to scrounge for data. The columnist need never leave the office.

And even those without legmen have an army of unpaid informants to help fill their columns. These poop procurers go by many names: press agents, public-relations counselors, PR men, media advisers . . . but behind their backs you'll call them flacks.

Today all celebrities, not just show-biz stars, have flacks. Sports teams have them, corporate bigwigs have them, military officers and prelates have them, the president of the United States has them. A flack's job is to get his client's name in the papers. If you're a gossip columnist, you don't have to call a flack; he calls you.

Or writes. Every day, flacks will drop you a ton or two of press releases to alert the world to their clients' latest achievements. Some of the larger flack firms employ special workers called planters whose only function is to feed the gossip columns. The planter passes you nasty dirt on celebrity nonclients; in payment, you print a few innocuous positive items about clients.

And that's only part of the free fodder you'll receive. Restaurant and club owners will tip you off on which celebrities frequent their establishments. Helpful malicious scum will give you unsolicited dirt on their enemies. You'll also be viewing the important new movies, TV shows, books, and magazines before they hit the theaters, stores, and newsstands. Don't worry; the flacks will make sure of it. You'll be inundated with advance copies and invitations to screenings and previews. In this era of infotainment, writing about what someone else has written or created counts as news. On a slow day, you can fill half your column with quotes from a forthcoming magazine article or descriptions of "sizzling" (as you will invariably call them) scenes from some mediocre movie about to open. Your readers, who can't see the movie for several weeks, will consider you a well-connected, savvy insider. They'd kill to be you.

But always remember: In a gossip column, what you say is not as important as *whom* you say.

The name's the game. That is why the names are in boldface.

So readers can skim the column, slowing only for the boldfaces who interest them. The more hot names in your column, the hotter the column. If Madonna is the megastar of the moment, you *must* give Madonna multiple mentions. It does not—and Media Person cannot emphasize this strongly enough—*it does not matter in the least what you say about her*.

One of America's best-known society-gossip columnists, Aileen Mehle, professionally known as Suzy, is notorious for writing columns that are largely lists of celebrities who attended parties the night before. "Among the guests were," writes Suzy in her dazzling style, and then drops a ton of boldface on you. Her own attendance is not strictly mandatory, as was embarrassingly revealed by a rival columnist who caused a minor sensation by noting that one party Suzy described had taken place after she wrote the column and several boldfaces on her list never attended.

The most sophisticated method of gossip-column name-dropping is to not mention the name at all. All you drop is a hint. This classic technique is known as the blind item. Used sparingly, it is tantalizingly powerful.

What high-profile, glamoroso Tinseltown twosome is on the verge of splitsville?

The reader has no idea but is dying to find out. Of course you have no idea either, since you made the thing up. But since some Tinseltown twosome is *always* on the verge of splitsville, there's bound to be a breakup before the week is out and then you can spend several paragraphs bragging about how you scooped the world.

Bragging is essential. If you don't constantly pat yourself on the back, readers will sense that you are not really a top gossip columnist and desert you for a more boastful rival.

You must read your rivals too, because they are a rich source of copy. Whatever the competition asserts, you can deny. This not only gets you a cheap scoop but makes you look more knowing. A typical denial item:

No, **Madonna** was NOT playing kissy-face with **Dan Quayle** at the Beverly Hills McDonald's in the wee hours, as **Liz Smith** boo-booed yesterday. That was a LOOKALIKE. The hot skinny is the blond bomb-shell was home in bed with la grippe all night . . . ALONE!!!

Note carefully the exceedingly hideous writing in the previous paragraph because that is the most important element of the gossip art. To be a truly successful gossip columnist, you must learn to be the worst writer you can. Fortunately this is easy to achieve today. The collapse of the American educational system ensures our future supply of gossip columnists.

Bad writing subliminally perpetuates the myth that the gossip columnist spends all her time racing around town poking into garbage cans, peering into windows, bribing doormen and waiters and plying brokenhearted ex-lovers of stars with drink before dart-ing back to the office with seconds to spare and rattling off a hot sheaf of scalding scandal in breathless if not deathless prose.

Pepper your copy with clichés, dated slang, mixed metaphors, lurid banalities, and grotesque punctuation, and readers will sense that you're a hard-driving dynamo with no time for literary nice-ties. Of course in truth you're a bloated parasite sitting around the office lazily collating offerings from flacks, handouts, and legmen. But you're a very rich, happy parasite.

Oh, yes—cornball sentimentality, false pieties, pompous plati-tudes, and sappy patriotic blather are also helpful, as well as a touch of smarmy cynicism. But no real wit, please. Bitchiness is fine, as long as you're just vindictive and never truly funny.

Here are a few helpful tips to start you down the road to bad writing, so essential for your successful gossip career:

Never allow anyone to work for a living: Billy Boldface *toils* for Paramount.

No one writes a book. They *scribble* a *tome* or better yet, *pen a tell-all sizzler*.

Singers don't sing. They *warble*.

Please, no money. What stars earn is *green stuff* or *major bucks*. What do they have to do to get the green stuff? They *ink* a *pact*.

Any large amount of money (the only kind you'll ever write about) must be preceded by the word *cool*. For some inexplicable reason, writing "half a million dollars" or "$500,000" impresses no one. But make it *a cool half mil* and readers everywhere slap their foreheads and exclaim, "Woweee, that's major bucks!" Gossip columnists have to know such things.

Elizabeth Taylor must always be referred to as *the violet-eyed beauty*. This is mandatory. She should not wear jewels but *drip with diamonds*. Tom Cruise and similar *hunks* must have the phrase *heartthrob* placed before their name.

Newspaper people must be identified as *ink-stained wretches*. True gossip columnists find this chestnut irresistibly funny. Lawyers are *legal eagles*.

There is no such thing as a corporate president. It's *prexy*.

People don't die. They *perish*. People don't fly. They *wing to the coast*. They don't go home but to their *digs*. They go not to bars, saloons, pubs, or lounges but to *watering holes*.

No one suffers embarrassment. They are *red-faced*. Towns are *abuzz* with rumors.

Any group of more than one actor is *a star-studded Hollywood cast*. The correct lead for any social event at which two or more actors will be present is: *The stars will be out tonight*.

Are you taking notes? In general, the thing to remember is never use an ordinary word when you can use a "colorful" word, painfully strained and corny though it may seem at first. Lose that elitist sensibility of yours. Instead of talk-show host, say *gab* host. Instead of legs, *gams* or *wheels* or . . . anything, really, except legs.

Now some stylistic pointers to shoot your gossip column to the top: Use many exclamation points to signal the reader how exciting your material is. The word FLASH! also helps. Use nicknames to show that you're an intimate of the stars, not just some ordinary news drudge. If you don't know the nicknames, make them up. Soon the star will be answering to your handle. This is the power of the media. Put "quotation marks" around words and "phrases" that don't really "need" them to show that you're capable of being hiply "ironic."

Okay, that's enough. Hold on. Stop the chapter. Something just occurred to Media Person: Why is he wasting his time giving you all this free advice when he could become a gossip columnist and get rich himself?

Can You Learn French from Television?

There is something irresistible about French.

No one really knows why, but all English-speaking people have a deep-rooted desire to converse in this beautiful and quirky language, preferably while sitting on the terrace of a Paris café with a lovely fashion model, sipping a fine cognac. Many try, doomed though they are to fail. Even sadder are those who suffer the delusion that they *can* speak French.

You see evidence of this neurotic affliction whenever an American newspaper runs any kind of feature story involving France. Invariably the headline will break into French for a word or two, as if the writer were announcing: "See, I can too speak it if I want."

The New York Times gave in to the impulse frequently during the French Revolution bicentennial. One headline said:

1789, AVEC COOKIES AND MILK

Another read:

LIBERTÉ, WON AND LOST

When Charles Schulz was honored in Paris and a picture of Snoopy was hung in the Louvre, the *New York Daily News*, straining desperately for a Gallic touch, managed this:

SNOOPY'S LE TOP DOG

It was enough to make you *mal* to your stomach.

Media Person's own experience with this formidable tongue is typical. He diligently studied it for four years in high school and college. As a result, he left school totally unable to speak, read, or understand French.

Few Americans can, and Media Person has a theory to explain why. It is shocking but it must be told. Media Person believes that the French taught to foreigners and tourists is not French at all. It is faux French, a simplified, cutesified version that bears only a small resemblance to the language used by actual French people.

Faux French consists of short sentences and familiar words so easy to learn that even people with no formal instruction whatever can figure them out. Here is some typical faux French of the sort you can find in any tourist guidebook or classroom textbook:

La plume de ma tante est morte.
(My aunt's pen is dead.)

Voulez-vous couchez avec moi ce soir? Ouf! Vous avez me frappé dans le nez.
(Would you like to sleep with me tonight? Ow! You hit me in the nose.)

Regardez! Le chien de mon ami mange mon père.
(Look! My friend's dog is eating my father.)

That is not French. It is French Lite. You can memorize hundreds of such phrases and they are utterly useless. No Frenchman would be caught dead uttering or responding to sentences so obvious and straightforward. No Frenchwoman would ever use a faux word like *ami*, but would choose one of the hundreds of obscure slang variations available. Real Frenchmen converse in bursts of impenetrable idiom, arcane tenses, and grotesquely complex syntax supplemented with intricate gestures indecipherable to non-natives. Here is an example of true, authentic, no-kidding-around French as spoken in France (though minus the gestures):

Qu'est-ce que ça c'est laquelle qui ça coquelle que ceci est quèquille? Est-ce que là-bas c'est ça cacharille que cela parce que quenelles est là paräquillies de les quillieuquesez? Merde! Tant pis! Elles ne fût fuillé pas aucun d'aquoisitille de cela ou quoi m'a l'equipeuilli les pischapilles qui est pu dû vos parapouillions ouprimipareux à la Pouilly Fuissé. Qu'est-ce que c'est quoi vous quilliquoise, n'est-ce pas? Voilà! Pfui!

(You call this swill lunch?)

Why is faux French foisted on trusting, innocent foreigners? Media Person has no proof, but all evidence points to the probability that France is playing a little practical joke on the rest of the world. It must be quite droll, after all, watching some new arrival, eager to converse after eight years of studying what he thought was French, realize with sudden horror that he cannot understand anything being said to him.*

It could explain why the English fought the French for one hundred years and the Germans invaded them three times.

What got Media Person meditating on this conspiracy is that, for some reason, a number of French programs have begun to appear on his television set.

And Media Person, drawn by that old Gallic fatal attraction, tries to watch them, despite minimal comprehension.

Weeknights at seven, there is *Le Journal*, a half hour of news from Paris. It's similar to the American network news shows but seems to contain twice as much information. This is because (1) *Le Journal* lacks commercials and (2) the French speak twice as fast as we do, yet another idiosyncrasy making them impossible to understand.

Saturday afternoons comes *Apostrophes*, a show that has no real American equivalent. Apparently, *Apostrophes* is a big deal in

---

*Media Person suspects the entire conspiracy is being masterminded by the sinister and mysterious Académie Française, the august body of intellectuals that is supposedly the guardian of French culture but which in fact has no comprehensible function whatever.

France despite its bizarre subject matter. For an hour and fifteen minutes, talking heads prattle unashamedly on a topic banned from American television: books. Any American host flaunting bookishness as does Bernard Pivot, a man who usually has reading glasses sliding down his nose and who sometimes picks up a volume right in front of everybody and quotes from it unashamedly, would be assassinated and/or replaced by Deborah Norville.

(One memorable February afternoon, Media Person thought he understood a sentence he heard on *Apostrophes*. He'll never forget that day.)

Weekday mornings Media Person watches the most heartbreaking of them all, *French in Action*. This is the one he comes most poignantly close to understanding, perhaps because its whole point, its *raison d'être*—oops, sorry—is ostensibly to teach Media Person French.

French in Action is an extraordinary program. It consists of fifty-two half-hour shows, which the PBS station in New York keeps running over and over, one a day. Each opens with a ten-minute playlet, another episode in the continuing adventures of Robert and Mireille, an attractive young couple falling in love in Paris. Then comes the teacher with his daily lesson. He is Pierre J. Capretz, the Maurice Chevalier of pedagogues, an engaging, indefatigable man who created the series and stars in it.

Capretz speaks no English on the show. He reviews the Robert-and-Mireille episode, illustrating his points with props, music, puppets, a mime, photographs, cartoons, and snippets from French movies and TV commercials. He gives you not only language but cultural instruction so that you learn, for instance, that on Sundays everyone in France buys cake, and the rest of the week they sit in the café where Ernest Hemingway once drank (any café in France) and they argue about movies.

The whole thing is done with great humor, charm, and intelligence. It's the most painless educational exercise Media Person has ever seen and provides more entertainment value than many feature films, sitcoms, and game shows.

But does it work?

Well, every time Media Person has had a productive session with *French in Action,* he thinks, "Now I'm really getting somewhere," and goes to *Le Journal,* sure that at last he'll be able to sit back and listen to the evening news in French and comprehend it.

He understands about three words of it.

It would appear that Pierre J. Capretz has sprung on us the most devilishly subtle faux French joke in the tortured history of this vast conspiracy.

But despite the frustration, despite his dark suspicions, Media Person has a dream, a mad, romantic reverie that one day he will slip across the tantalizing threshold of comprehension. Suddenly the gibberish will unscramble. He will not only speak French— authentic, complicated, idiomatic French—he will *think* in French.

Then he will uproot and at last change his life. Completely. No more lying around all day reading *The New York Times* and watching *L.A. Law.* He will move to Paris, taking an airy apartment with a splendid view of the Seine. He'll lie on a *chaise longue* all day sipping *vin blanc*, reading *Le Monde* and *Le Canard Enchaîné*. He'll watch Eric Rohmer and Jerry Lewis on the VCR. Instead of being mystified and impressed by *Apostrophes,* he'll sneer at its pretentious bourgeois superficiality.

Everyone must have a dream. That much Media Person understands. But why does his have to be in French?

A Short, Pink
History of Fluff

It was noon when the flakes began falling. They were soft and pink and feathery light and soon Media Person was buried up to his scruffy beard.

"What the hell?" he whined just before sneezing eighty or ninety times in rapid succession. But even as he asked, he knew the frightening truth.

Fluff.

The U.S. had fluffed out. An unstoppable blizzard of fluff had engulfed the land, displacing all substance. It was irresistible. Media Person gave up any pretense of seriousness and frolicked in the swirling, frilly pinkness. He noticed that it twinkled, for there were occasional specks of glitz amid the fluff.

Soviet tanks bullied Lithuania, the yen plunged, but Media Person didn't care. He giggled and turned to the gossip columns and read all about Donald Trump and his wife and his mistress. He flipped from CNN to MTV and watched his giddy feet dance to the beat of the latest Madonna video.

In France, they say *la fleufe*. In Germany, *das pflaff*. In sunny

Italy, it's *flufaretto*. In Yiddish, *schmutz*. South of the border, it's *fluffada* and it swirls to the rhythm of the rhumba. Julius Caesar warned against *fluvum*, which could sap the virility of a nation if permitted to flourish unchecked. Fluff showed up in the drawings of Leonardo da Vinci, and medieval alchemists believed they could convert it from lint. If all the fluff in the world were laid flake to flake it would stretch from Andy Rooney all the way to Willard Scott.

But wait. What was this? Was the fluff turning green? Could it be? Was it turning into . . .

Broccoli! The president of the United States had issued a fluffoid statement and the press was fluffing it up into major news.

BUSH BLASTS BROCCOLI

George (I'm the Prez and I'll Eat What I Want) Bush had taken a stand. Let the Democrats make of it what they would. Let the broccoli farmers eat cake.

What Bush craves is pork rinds and beef jerky, ice cream and popcorn. His predecessor, Reagan, was famous for jelly beans. His, Carter, was Mr. Peanut. What is the larger significance of these puerile habits? Simple. Such foods are nutritional fluff. Fluff starts at the top.

The press devoted many fluffy paragraphs to the broccoli issue. *The New York Times* informed its readers that Bush "eats with a shoveling motion, bent over his plate, sometimes sticking his napkin into his shirt like a bib so he won't soil his shirt and tie."

Media Person bent over his newspaper and ate up this fluff. His appetite for it was limitless. He skipped a *Times* editorial on how America's entire political system has gone totally haywire. Sounded too significant. Instead he greedily devoured an editorial on *Symplocarpus foetidus*: skunk cabbage.

He turned to the world of science and found a fabulous article on Gloria Estefan's aching back. The popular singer had been in a bus crash and Media Person scooped up every morsel. He learned that to realign her fractured vertebrae and straighten the "kinked" spinal cord, her orthopedic surgeon permanently attached two one-quarter-inch-diameter surgical-steel rods to the back of Gloria's spine, using eight hooks on each! By God, it was classic pop-medical-media fluff.

DOCS SAY PLUCKY POP STAR WILL DANCE AGAIN!

Media Person decided to do the *Times* Sunday crossword. Previously this might have entailed some slight amount of thinking. But no more. Not in the fabulous age of fluff. Now you just dial 1-900-884-CLUE. For seventy-five cents for the first minute and fifty cents for each additional minute, you get three answers. Media Person called forty-six times, got all 148 answers, and solved the puzzle in record time. Worry about the bill later. Isn't it grand to be living in such an era of progress?

Media Person felt a warm sense of fluffilment.

Fluff was flying out of the newspapers.

There was:

Medical fluff: A German woman sued an aviation company for twenty thousand dollars, Media Person read, because pressure from a low-flying jet fighter plane caused her silicone cheek implants to explode.

Fluff menace: Ann Landers warned readers to keep their toilet lids down. Parrots, cats, dogs, and children sometimes fall in and drown.

Historic, heroic fluff from exotic, far-off lands: Genghis Khan, Media Person read, is hot again! Mongolians now see him as a national hero. There are two hit songs named after him and a vodka too.

Fashion fluff (a redundancy, of course): Ungaro, the Prince of Prints, was featuring blasts of startling, wake-up colors and skirts that are sexy, short, and tight, Media Person read. Ungaro said his prints are "nonviolent." *USA Today* said "they shout but never scream."

Media Person looked at his own clothes with dismay. They weren't fluffy enough. They didn't shout or scream. They just sort of sat there and whimpered. Media Person would have to get noisier clothing.

Or maybe he could just chant a fluff rap!

Man I need my fluff
It's the finest stuff now I wouldn't bluff
But things was rough and I couldn't get enough.
I was hurtin' bad I was startin' to suffer
Then I thought of my pillow, hey, it couldn't be fluffer.
So I puffed it up and ripped out the stuffin'
Smoked it all but I didn't feel nuffin'!

Media Person turned on the radio for some verbal fluff and on came Larry King. But wait, here was trouble. He had a nonfluff guest, the biographer Robert Caro. Uh-oh. People were calling in with intelligent questions about Lyndon Johnson and Texas politics. Media Person thought for one desperate moment that he might have to change stations. Then it happened. A caller asked the distinguished author: "Mr. Caro, who do you think would win a battle of wits, Larry King or Howard Stern?"

Fluff! It'll get ya every time.

It's always out there, waiting. Just waiting. Then, suddenly, it sees its chance and it . . . *wafts*. And you are enfluffed.

Face it. This is our destiny, our life, our passion. We are in fluff's thrall now and forever. America, go fluff yourself.

I Hear America Munching

In the spring of 1988 a bizarre affliction befell the *New York Daily News*, then America's largest general-circulation daily newspaper.

For no known reason, the *Daily News* fell madly in love with the word *munch*. Suddenly, munching ran amok in its columns, turning up in all parts of the paper.

Media Person first noticed the condition while reading a story about a disturbed woman who'd broken into David Letterman's home in Connecticut and tried to pass herself off to investigating police as the comedian's wife. The *Daily News* said that "the frail mystery woman" (newspapers love dopey phrases like that) had been "munching canned fruit."

It seemed unlikely, unless she'd been chewing on the can as well. *Munch* is a perfectly decent, authentic English word found in most dictionaries, but the *Daily News* didn't seem to understand its meaning, which is: to eat with a crunching sound.

That was only the beginning. A food column on sardines asked why more Americans aren't "munching more of these fabulous little fish."

A columnist at a political convention had Republicans "munching away" at a political breakfast. A reporter covering Ed Koch's mayoral campaign watched him eating street food and wrote, "Koch bought a dog from Pevodes Antonosio and munched."

Two paragraphs later, the story continued:

" 'MAYOR,' she yelled above a pack of reporters watching the mayor munch."

Maybe it wasn't a hot dog, as Media Person assumed, but a real dog, with bones intact.

Finally, munchomania spread even to the *News'* comics pages. A character in "Mother Goose," devouring a plate of *powdered doughnuts*, went "MUNCH MUNCH MUNCH."

Extremely stale doughnuts?

It was clear to Media Person that some terrible madness had overtaken the newspaper, something that went beyond the usual delusion of tabloid hacks that good, everyday words are somehow colorless and must be replaced at all costs by jazzy synonyms. Perhaps it was a phobic dread of the word *eat*, perhaps some mass hysteria, traceable to the company cafeteria, that had generated a fear of finding ground glass in one's food, so that *News* personnel imagined a crunching noise wherever there was chewing.

Obviously, counseling was desperately needed and it seemed to Media Person that the woman for the job was Dr. Joyce Brothers, America's number-one newspaper shrink. Otherwise, Media Person feared, this grotesque illness might munch through the sanity of the whole staff, reducing it to a rabble of tiny babbling munchkins without a shred of sanity.

The History of the Talk Show in America, Part I

Few people realize that the common, everyday talk show so familiar to American TV viewers has its roots in the opulent royal courts of Renaissance Europe.

The monarch on cushioned throne has evolved into the host on his couch, the colorful procession of peers, knights, and foreign envoys before the court has its counterpart in today's show-biz guests and the servile footmen and lackeys have become the sidekick announcers and bandleaders of modern times.

At least that's the theory Media Person has been pushing, though mainstream historians have been painfully slow to ratify, or even notice it.*

Fast-forwarding to twentieth-century America, we pause at the image of perhaps the greatest influence on the modern-day talk

---

*No scholar has yet discredited Media Person's monograph, *Early Sidekick Manifestations in the European Courts*, which revealed that King Henry VIII employed a retainer whose job was to watch for the monarch's arrival and yell, "Heeeeeere's Henry!"

show, Arthur Godfrey. Indeed, some experts consider Godfrey the father of the talk show, though many others refuse to concede greatness to a man who insisted on playing a ukulele.

At the time, no one could figure out what, exactly, Godfrey's talent was. He wasn't really a comedian or singer, though he dabbled in those crafts. The less said about his musicianship the better. But now, more than forty years after the start of his morning radio program, it's obvious. Arthur Godfrey was a host. He brought out the talent and kidded around with them and somehow pleasantly frittered away hours and hours of our lives that could have been spent productively.

He may well have invented such talk-show necessities as ad-libbing, informality, and even sitting down, though it all happened so long ago that no one can ever be certain.

Informality? Godfrey was so informal that his studio audience was served lunch—*during the show*. Godfrey would sit there yacking and strumming against a background hubbub of people unwrapping salamis or chicken sandwiches, then chewing, slurping, and making other satisfied little eating sounds. Now that was a *host*. From today's talk-show kings, you get only talk.

But the sons and daughters of Godfrey have graced the ever-expandable form with many new enhancements.

Steve Allen pioneered the use of intelligent silliness, later perfected by David Letterman, the man who gave America the Stupid Pet Trick.

Jack Paar was the first to utilize the technique of bursting into tears and walking off the show in a huff. Another innovation of his—fascinating, witty, articulate guests—unfortunately fell into disuse.

Joan Rivers proved that the versatile talk-show format could accommodate a screeching, prying yenta.

Phil Donahue showed that talk shows could be more than a place for lighthearted fluff. They could also be a forum for serious issues, such as Transvestites Who Have Had Sex with Their Pets.

Oprah Winfrey demonstrated that a black woman could do anything Phil Donahue does.

(Oprah once stated: "The Bible's got every answer to every question that man could ever pose." This caused Media Person to wonder: Then why do we need her show?)

Mike Douglas and Merv Griffin developed blandness to such a point of perfection that there was absolutely no difference between their shows' being on the air and off.

Media Person isn't sure what new wrinkle Johnny Carson brought to the talk show but he kept bringing it longer than anyone else.

Dick Cavett showed that there is a place on television for arch, self-conscious, intellectual talk-show hosts. That place is cable. Also, a guest once dropped dead on Cavett's show, which was a talk-show first, or possibly a last.

Arsenio Hall is the most recent talk-show host to burst into popularity and therefore gets his own chapter because in Show-Biz America, new is better.

The History of the Talk Show in America, Part II

Time loves Arsenio Hall. *Time* thinks he's hip. Said so right on the cover. "TV's Hip Host Grabs the Post-Carson Generation."

"Huh?" said Media Person (who's been talking to himself a lot lately). "This guy's hip?"

Arsenio is young and black and spouts authentic African-American teenage slang, or what sounds like it to Media Person's untrained ear. Give him hipness points for all that.

Arsenio sometimes amuses. He has high energy and whips up a party atmosphere that some find exciting. His studio audiences find it so exciting they *bark*.

Media Person isn't sure whether barking or, more precisely, woofing, is hip but deep down in the inner recesses of his soul, he doubts it. For dogs, yes.

Only half a point can be awarded for the fact that Arsenio is more comfortable than Carson or Letterman asking guest starlets about their sex lives. So are Donahue, Winfrey, and Sally Jessy Raphael. So's your grandma.

Big demerits must be issued for three serious offenses against hip:

1. Breast-pocket handkerchiefs. (*Ed McMahon* wears them, for heaven's sake.)
2. The very fact that *Time* finds Hall hip. What could be more damning evidence of unhip? "Man, this show is loose!" proclaimed the far-out hepcats who write and edit America's grooviest newsmagazine.*
3. The Sandy Duncan Suck-Up Syndrome. One depressing evening, Media Person saw Arsenio Hall interview Sandy Duncan. He not only appeared genuinely interested in Sandy Duncan's hideously typical network sitcom, the name of which escapes Media Person, but asked her questions indicating that he *actually watched* said sitcom, perhaps regularly.

Can such as this truly be a man of hip? Or just a man of jive?

Sucking up to the Sandy Duncans of the world is what Merv Griffin and Mike Douglas used to do in the bleak era before Letterman made it clear that a talk-show host's sacred duty is ridiculing the guest's bad sitcom (Letterman would always ask Susan St. James of *Kate and Allie*, "Are you Kate or Allie?") and sniping at, not enhancing, phony show-biz hype.

Isn't Arsenio just Merv with a posse?†

Does hip mean only up-to-the-minute trendiness? Or does it require an attitude involving some degree of opposition to the prevailing ethos? Isn't hipness largely about being an outsider? Arsenio doesn't seem like one, even though he's new to stardom, a member of an ethnic minority, and is seen by *Time* as a breakthrough for funk (a subdivision of hip). To Media Person he looks like a comfortable member of Club Show Biz.

Or does all this carrying on about hip just prove that Media Person is hopelessly unhip?

Actually, Media Person suspects that hipness itself is unhip. If

---

*In its definitive article on rap, *Time* attempted to quote DJ Jazzy Jeff and the Fresh Prince but incorrectly rendered the phrase "gettin' dissed" (which even Raisa Gorbachev knows is short for "receiving disrespect") as "gettin' *dished*," another plate of beans entirely.

†One of the many hip words Arsenio uses.

mass-market *Time* sees itself as an arbiter of hip, then its zillions of readers are hip. But since *Time*'s readers are by definition unhip, then hip has become meaningless.

What you get now is mere trendiness posing as hip.

Arsenio Hall provides the illusion rather than the real thing. This would put him squarely, so to speak, in the tradition of the late Sammy Davis, Jr. He's *faux* hip.

Uh-oh, Media Person is afraid he's onto a hot media idea now. Faux Hip: Trend of the '90s! Let a thousand magazine articles bloom.

Listen, Media Person is sorry. Forget he ever brought this whole thing up. Let's just get to the next chapter.

Name That Goon

Sometimes Media Person gets confused reading the crime news because the newspapers can't get the nicknames of the criminals straight.

When an unpleasant maniac began terrorizing the A train in the New York subway system, one paper quickly named him The Psycho Straphanger. But another called him The Piper, which referred not to a musical instrument but his weapon of choice.

Clearly the first effort, with its alliteration and general raffishness, was superior. But both were preferable to what *The New York Times* called him: "A man who randomly attacked at least six people with metal pipes during rush hour subway rides in Queens, Brooklyn and Manhattan."

The *Times* never seems able to enter properly into the spirit of these things.

Curiously no headline writer took into account the colorful fact that the maniac always stared menacingly at his victim before attacking. This could have led to such creative names as The A-Train Eyeballer or The Silently Stalking, Stonily Staring, and Suddenly Striking Psycho Straphanger.

Next the *Daily News* named a criminal terrorizing old people in their homes The Midnight Caller and the *Post* tagged another murderous felon The Slasher but no one else picked up on either alias.

It's a curious feature of criminality that Mafia members handle their own nicknames but in the case of other offenders, the job falls to the media. Media Person supposes this is one of the advantages of being in organized crime.

What we really need is someone to take charge of nicknaming the major perpetrators, a moniker monitor. Maybe there could be one in each state, appointed by the governor. Otherwise, with so many police sketches filling the newspapers, how is an eyewitness supposed to report a felon to the authorities without causing terrible confusion?

"Hey, I've spotted The Stinky Strangler," a 911 dialer might say.

"What?" the police dispatcher might reply. "I don't know about any Stinky Stranger. You mean The Chortling Choker?"

"Uh, gee, I don't know. I'm not close enough to tell if the guy is laughing or smells bad but he's definitely strangling someone."

"Well, I'll send a car around to check, but it doesn't really sound like the guy we're looking for."

It's exactly this type of situation that Media Person's proposal would prevent in the future.

Senseless Headline in Brainless Tabloid

We all have our obsessions, and Media Person's is the *New York Post*. It is the main function of this mendacious newspaper to provide Media Person's daily anger fix, without which he has no means of knowing whether or not he's alive.

Let us examine in detail the history of a fascinating New York institution:

1. The *Post* was founded in 1801 by Alexander Hamilton. This makes it, according to most authorities, the oldest continuously published newspaper in the U.S.
2. It remained normal until 1977, when purchased by voracious media eater Rupert Murdoch, and for the next eleven years was a boiling stew of mayhem, gore, sex, fiction, and hard right-wing politics. Today it has calmed down, but not much.
3. No one cares about the rest.

    Much can be said about the *Post*, most of it bad, but in one vital area the *Post* has ruled for more than a decade: the headline.

The loud, sassy tabloid head is an art form, or at least pop art. The finest examples approach the realm of haiku. Miracles of compression, headlines embody the whole challenge of tabloid journalism—to say a lot in a small space. And, no less important, to grab the reader—and slap him around till he coughs up some change. That's necessary because tabloids depend heavily on newsstand sales.

Before the Murdoch era at the *Post*, it was usually the *Daily News* that produced memorable banners in New York City. Its best-remembered effort was the exquisite 1976 masterpiece

FORD TO NY:

DROP DEAD

which suffered not a bit from the fact that Gerald Ford had never actually uttered the rancid slur. In a tabloid banner, it's the spirit that counts. New York was going broke, the president was clearly not rushing to the rescue, and the *News* caught the moment with acerb wit.

But somehow the *News* lost its heads and the *Post*, now populated by raffish madmen from Australia, found them. Here was the classic immigrant struggle all over again: hungry newcomers yearning to make their mark, only this time all over the front page of a major newspaper.

The second most famous banner of the Murdoch Era emerged from the capture of David Berkowitz, a quiet, polite young psychotic who spent his spare time skulking around New York shooting people and writing notes to the police signed Son of Sam until he was nabbed and sedated for several decades. After his arrest, the *Post* managed to get a jailhouse photo of Berkowitz asleep on a cot in his cell. It ran the photo big—on page one, of course, as Berkowitz recumbent was the most important thing going on in the world that day—under the memorable legend

SAM SLEEPS

It was a statement at once mysteriously eloquent and profoundly stupid. Thousands cheered. But the banner that will forever live in journalistic glory as the shining moment of the venerable *Post* was the one that appeared above the account of a grisly but otherwise forgettable murder story.

Its greatness was such that its creator, an obscure deskman, escaped the usual fate of the drudges who write headlines: anonymity. When the *Post* promoted him five years later, it ran a proud story that began:

V. A. Musetto, author of the most famous headline in the New York *Post*'s 189-year history, has been named the paper's Arts & Leisure editor.

It was in 1983 that Musetto wrote the work that gave him immortality:

HEADLESS BODY IN TOPLESS BAR

The grandeur of this big-type classic with its brilliant, semipoetic repetition of the suffix *less* proved once again the old axiom that more less is more.

More or less.

The Murdoch Era at the *Post* ended, at least in a technical sense, in 1988 when the paper was sold to a real-estate mogul named Peter Kalikow, who specialized in kicking elderly and modest-income people out of their apartments and converting the buildings into luxury co-ops for the wealthy. Such a man was well qualified to continue the Murdoch tradition of championing the rich, powerful, and well-connected. Kalikow did not mind losing tens of millions of dollars a year on the *Post* because it was a pittance to him and because being a press lord got him invited to more interesting parties as well as black-tie dinners at which plaques were presented to him as a humanitarian.

Kalikow eventually handed editorial control to Jerry Nachman, an energetic television newsman who personified the tabloid mentality: print first, check later. Nachman's *Post*, for example, would report that the New York Mets had fired their manager, Davey Johnson, with a page-one banner that screamed:

YER OUT!

Pedantic quibbles to the effect that the Mets hadn't, in fact, fired Johnson were fortunately not allowed to stand in the way of this exciting story. After all, he *was* fired a year later; so the *Post* was out in front of everyone.

Nachman also wrote a column for the *Post*. It wasn't a bad column, but it had a subtext that frequently rendered it hilarious. Nachman, a blimp of a man, was unable to disguise an obsession with his own alimentary canal and that which courses through it. Any time he required a figure of speech, he would go with his gut instinct.

Once, addressing a city ambulance shortage, he opened with:

You just think about it, the next time you step outside after that too heavy lunch. Maybe it's a queasy rumble in your stomach or a stab of heartburn that won't go away.

In another column, Nachman was analyzing the case of Stanley Friedman, a Bronx politician jailed for corruption. Nachman tried mightily to stick to the subject, but what kept sneaking in unbidden was his desperate need for a nosh.

Forget about "country club prisons." The decision you made last Sunday on whether to go out for brunch or bring bagels home is a pretty good definition of liberty.

A few paragraphs later, with Nachman's fantasy brunch apparently having progressed from bagels to lox and sturgeon, he demanded: "What big fish can Stanley Friedman give up?"

But the finest Snackman passage, one that ranged subliminally across the entire digestive process (albeit in reverse), came when he tried to vividly explain to his readers the painful daily struggle faced by newspaper columnists:

It is a private world of torture, a constipated man grunting. That's why columns are not written in concert halls for all to see. It is like the description of sausage manufacture: You're better off not seeing how it's made if you want to enjoy the product.

Under Jerry Nachman, the *Post* continued to honor its solemn obligation to startle the jaded New Yorker in five words or less.

The great newspaper war that erupted in February 1990, when the media learned that the boastful billionaire Donald Trump had taken a mistress and become estranged from his highly publicized wife, Ivana, produced a bounty of memorable banners. But it was Nachman's *Post* that again won top honors.

In an article in the *Washington Journalism Review*, *Post* reporter Bill Hoffmann candidly recounted what it was like to be part of that thrilling time:

> We tossed out all the rules and wrote stirring sagas of lust and power and sex and betrayal. . . . After the third or fourth day there was no doubt about it—we had entered The Tabloid Zone. Fact, rumor and fiction began living together happily and could easily be mistaken for each other. But circulation soared. The public wanted more. My editors wanted more. And I wasn't about to disappoint them.

Carrying out his Tabloid Zone duties, Hoffmann made contact with a friend of Marla Maples, the Other Woman in the Trump triangle. The public already knew much about Maples, thanks to Hoffmann and his cliché-spewing colleagues. It knew that she was a blond sexpot, a blond bombshell, a buxom blonde, a busty beauty, a curvy starlet, and a stunner. But now the friend Hoffmann had dug up blabbed something even more significant: Maples's analysis of coitus with Donald. Their conjugation brought about the birth of another unforgettable *Post* banner:

"BEST SEX I'VE EVER HAD"

Hoffmann, no fool, knew it was the best news he'd ever had. He wrote: "As soon as I heard that, I thought, BINGO!"

But under Jerry Nachman, the *Post* was not content to grind out one-shot banners, barn-burners though they might be. It also invented a whole new genre of headline. Media Person refers, of course, to the Belching Banner, a blinding explosion of pure feeling.

BASTARDS!

screamed the *Post* in August 1988, when some terrorists in Lebanon hanged a hostage. A new journalistic form had been born. Previously headlines were thought to exist for the purpose of telling the reader what had happened. But now the *Post* had redefined that function into *disapproving* of what had happened and casting blame.

A few days later, when the terrorists made public a videotape showing the victim hanging, the *Post* followed up with

GHOULS

Shortly after a Bronx after-hours social club was set on fire, killing eighty-seven people, police arrested a young man who was angry with a woman who worked at the club. The *Post* front page belched:

THE MONSTER

Media Person became very excited as he realized the magnitude of the *Post*'s breakthrough. The Belching Banner answered a greatly felt need. Constantly forced to write about terrible people doing awful things, journalists grow frustrated. They can only keep describing the horror, never do anything about it. But now the *Post* had discovered that you could do something after all. You could call the bad guys names. Sure, it doesn't stop the terror and destruction that mar our modern world, but at least it makes the journalist feel better. And isn't that why people become journalists in the first place?

And rage was not the only emotion a belching banner could summon up. By June 1990, the *Post* had developed the capacity to register disgust, as with the belcher it ran over the photo of a man slogging through the goo that befouled the New Jersey shoreline after an oil spill:

YUCK!

When comedian Roseanne Barr caused a two-day tabloid sensation by screeching and wailing the National Anthem before a baseball game in San Diego, the *Post*'s front page screeched and wailed:

NOW YOU CAN CALL HER ROSEANNE . . .
BARR-F!

Media Person braced himself for the inevitable onslaught of Belching Banners as other newspapers and magazines caught on. Soon, he thought, a person walking past a newsstand would have to cringe as epithets like Louse! Scurvy Swine! and Ratfink! leapt out to assault the eye, or even

FILTHY ROTTEN NO-GOOD SCUM-SUCKING CREEP!

In particular, Media Person was concerned for Leona Helmsley, on trial for income-tax evasion. The hotel queen's Marie-Antoinette-like image already had aroused great antipathy from public and media alike. Media Person figured it was only a matter of time till she fell victim to a Belching Banner.

Soon enough she did. Fortunately for Helmsley, it was not a tough tabloid like the *Post* that belched her, but a news magazine. Attempting the tricky form for the first time, the timid gents of *Newsweek* simply could not bring themselves to blurt the angry term they yearned to, but could only coyly proffer:

RHYMES WITH RICH

Despite the large photo of Helmsley, many readers doubtless were stumped and had to call in for hints from blushing editors. "Snitch?" Media Person could imagine them querying. "Witch?" Media Person predicted that *Newsweek*'s next rhymer would be a George Steinbrenner coverline:

SIMILAR TO A CRASS TROLL

But Media Person, as so often happens, was disappointed.

An Embarrassment of Niches

You know how many new magazines come out every year? *Six hundred.* Media Person just read that in a new magazine.

Long ago, when Media Person was Media Tot, America was a simple, God-fearing country that needed damned few magazines because everyone was always out planting corn and fighting grizzly bears. In your home, you had *Life* or the *Saturday Evening Post* or the *Reader's Digest*. Down at the barbershop or the beauty parlor you might find *Field & Stream*, *Popular Mechanics*, or *Ladies' Home Journal*. If you knew some degenerate, pointy-headed intellectual, he might read *Time*. That was it. There may have been other magazines, but decent folk had no use for them.

Then America got weird.

In the '60s and '70s, the magazine population expanded. In the '80s, it exploded. Now it is totally out of control. There are so many magazines the newsstands are bursting and yet every week new ones come out.

Every city now has its own magazine, every sport, every hobby. Computers alone have spawned hundreds of magazines. Every demographic group is represented, every interest, every sexual variety. There's a magazine devoted to *Arizona Highways*. Dating practices among unmarried young blacks is the topic of *Chocolate Singles*. Are you a woman? There is *Working Woman* for working women, *Working Mother* for working women with children, *New York Woman* for New York women, *Savvy Woman* for women no one can fool. Did you recently become a woman? There is *New Woman*. Have you been one for a long time? *Lear's*. Are you a French woman? *Elle*. Black woman? *Essence*. Hispanic woman? *Imagen*. Fashionable woman? *Vogue* or *Glamour* or *Mirabella*. *Seventeen* and *Sassy* cover teenage women. *Playboy* and *Penthouse* uncover women.

Interested in business and finance? Take your pick of *Business Week*, *Business Month*, *Forbes*, *Fortune*, *Financial World*, *Global Finance*, *Money*, *Corporate Finance, Inc.*, or *Manhattan Inc.*, and that's not to mention business newspapers like *Barron's* or *Investor's Daily*.

If you're feeling a little dumb, you could read *Smart* and if you're feeling a little dim, you could read *Fame*. When *Fame* appeared in 1988, the editors proudly proclaimed that it "glows with a brightness level of 80 and opacity of 90—the highest attainable quality for any magazine of this type." Here at last was the magazine for coal miners and anyone caught in a power blackout.

Who on earth reads all these magazines? Media Person's theory is: nobody. The concept being followed is called "niche marketing." Publishers believe that a niche magazine can be targeted at a small, specialized group of people who can be sold to advertisers whose products appeal to that group. But so many copycat magazines were created that all the niches are stuffed to the bursting point.

Now Media Person is watching for the ultimate niche magazine: *Leonard J. Podgorski Weekly* will be exclusively devoted to news, photos, features, and commentary on Leonard J. Podgorski. You won't read it. You'll have your own.

What all this magazine madness has turned into is a gigantic shell game in which the trend-happy advertisers pour their money into the new "hot book" of the moment and enterprising publishers keep inventing new ones to excite them. Eventually the whole overinflated shebang will collapse like the Dutch tulip mania of the seventeenth century.

This will be the Great Magazine Crash* and it will be devastating. Distraught editors and publishers will leap into the presses to be stapled to death. Acres of bare newsstand racks will lie bleached in the sun.

Meanwhile, with the economy starting to contract, the existing magazines grow ever more desperate for attention. To stand out from the crowd, editors and advertisers will do almost anything. Picking up a magazine today has become a dangerous experience. Things leap out and attack you. Choking clouds of perfume spew from the pages, often asphyxiating asthmatics and others sensitive to toxic substances, pop-up ads explode in your face, sound effects generated by ingenious micro-batteries hammer your ears and "blow-in" subscription cards litter your floor like autumn leaves.

Gimmicks proliferate. *Spin* enclosed a free condom, allegedly to impress upon its readers the need for safe sex.

Bride's Magazine perpetrated a 1,040-page monstrosity that it called "the largest consumer magazine ever published." Most dangerous too. After picking it up, numerous brides had to be married in traction.

In fact, magazines have become so hazardous that Media Person advises prospective readers to take precautions: Wear a helmet, protective body armor, and safety glasses before opening any new publication.

Better yet, hire someone to prebrowse it for you. Why put yourself in needless danger? Media Person himself is occasionally available for this service. (Rates available on request.)

---

*Should the Great Magazine Crash come before Media Person can get this book into the stores—and a couple of magazines mentioned in this chapter have already folded even as Media Person was sitting here writing this footnote— remember, he first predicted the crash in 1989 and can prove it. Read his clips.

Fight Stress
the Cliché Way

Language, humankind's greatest invention, was developed to help people more effectively hide the truth from each other.

And one of the most popular tools of language is the cliché, a device gratefully employed by all mainstream news organizations.

In fact, it sometimes seems as though the media's main purpose is to distribute clichés to all members of the populace.

Perhaps by clothing the news in clichés, newswriters are unconsciously trying to reassure us (and themselves) that life is orderly, rational, and safe instead of the mad whirlpool of random, uncontrollable, tragicomic chaos it really is.

Or maybe they're just lazy. Abandoning clichés would force them to communicate in fresh, vigorous bursts of language. This would require thinking, which is hard and would make newsies even more tense and irritable than they already are, and finally their spouses and children would rebel and insist that they go back to clichés.

So in a vain attempt to fight stress, they keep writing the same stories over and over in the same words.

Indeed there are some newspeople who communicate exclusively through clichés. The *New York Daily News* columnist Richard G. Carter is a veritable titan of the trite. In one short column, he was able to work in "pet peeve," "worth his salt," "wet behind the ears," "the wool being pulled over their eyes," "you get the picture," and "I'm mad as hell, and I'm not going to take it anymore." In an even more impressive column, he managed "stop, look and listen," "brought down the house," "ruled the roost," "no mean feat," "in a class by herself," "alive and well," "[her] star was shining bright," and—twice—"the one and only."

Like everything else, styles in clichés change. Clichés used to be, by definition, old. Once a solid, well-built cliché of the kind favored by Richard G. Carter was passed down from generation to generation and never wore out. But in today's trendy media society, clichés come and go as quickly as pop songs. One season, everyone is saying "no way" or "give me a break" or "totally awesome." Then, just as suddenly, they're gone and every American child is saying "get a life."

Plagues of instant clichés sweep the media, dulling the brain and wincing the face. In 1988, an infantile expression once used only when dealing with babies completely captured public discourse in America. Columnist Erma Bombeck wrote: "We are not afraid to use the *d* word and talk about death." A headline in *Money* magazine said: "Marriage and the Other 'M' Word—Money." *The New Yorker*, referring to nuclear meltdowns, said: "The 'm' word is used rather freely these days." A right-wing columnist demanded: "What about Jesse Jackson and the 'c' word—communism?" A *New York Times* editorial-page feature on zucchini was headlined "The Z Word."

Media Person was beginning to be afflicted with the *n* word—nausea.

One area completely dominated by instant clichés is the insult. There are no longer any jerks, dopes, clods, slobs, or creeps in America. Today such unhip gibes would be used only by a wimp, a nerd, a dweeb, a dork, a sleazeball, or a geek.

Insults, in fact, are no longer insults. They're now *cheap shots*.

Today, whenever someone receives criticism, no matter how accurate or justified, he is apt to whine, as the Republicans did after the 1988 vice-presidential debate when Lloyd Bentsen told the overreaching Dan Quayle that he was no Jack Kennedy, "Hey, that's a cheap shot." Why won't anyone ever admit to being decimated by an expensive shot?

There are even cliché noises and gestures. Years ago, crowds used to signal approval by applauding or, if particularly enthusiastic, whistling or shouting "Rah!" or "Yah!" or, hard as it is to believe, "Hip, hip, hooray!" Today they slap each other's palms, emit falsetto whoops, or, in the case of studio audiences at certain television shows, bark like dogs.

There are also cliché ideas. These turn up on days when columnists run out of new ideas. You're then likely to encounter the following:

1. Baseball players make too much money.
2. Dan Quayle is not as dumb as people think (or, alternatively, is even dumber).
3. A reminiscence of the gruff but wise city editor who taught the columnist everything worth knowing back when he was a cub reporter.
4. Why can't TV weathermen predict the weather accurately?
5. "The Star-Spangled Banner" is a lousy national anthem.
6. Communism is just no damn good.*
7. Our tax system should be simplified.
8. Our taxes should be lowered.

And there are cliché photos. On July 11, 1988, in the midst of a summer heat wave, Media Person picked up a major American newspaper, *New York Newsday*, a proud member of the *Los Angeles Times* family, and almost fell off his couch.

There it was on page 1, an immense photograph, in color, of an

---

*This column was written so often that finally, even the communists came to believe it and converted to capitalism. So now there are no more communists, and yet the column is *still* being written.

egg. *An egg frying on the sidewalk*. The oldest, hoariest, mossiest, dreariest, dumbest cliché in all American photojournalism—and played perfectly straight, without even a trace of irony or redeeming self-hatred.

The TV news made for grim watching that night. All over town, citizens had seen the egg shot on the newsstands and crashed to the floor, pole-axed with disbelief, shattered at the thought of sharing the same city with a newspaper that could perpetrate something that embarrassing.

To this day, hardly anyone in New York ever buys *Newsday*.

How Come If Al's So Mean His Paper's So Bland?

A lot of people make fun of *USA Today* with its Technicolor graphics, life-size USA weather map, postcard-size stories, goofy pie charts,* and, of course, its relentless perkiness.

Unfortunately, Media Person is one of those people. He just can't help himself. It's too easy. Media Person has no discipline at all.

Of course it must be said in its defense that *USA Today* reporters often root out big stories the other papers miss. On one day, for example, the front page of "Money" (one of *USA*'s four main sections) ran a lengthy, chatty, *major* feature piece on the subject of *duct tape*. As if that weren't enough, on the same page, played even higher, was a story built around the amazing fact that July

*One of MP's favorites was "Democratic senators' favorite breads," which revealed that a huge majority of Democratic senators, 61 percent, preferred wheat breads. White, rye, and kaiser roll were tied with 9 percent each, 6 percent favored pumpernickel, and 6 percent liked "other." Another classic, "Pests feared most by men," disclosed that 2.8 percent of American males are scared of worms.

is a month with five paydays. Media Person saw these scoops nowhere else.

USA Today reached its greatest heights under its founder, Al Neuharth, the Gordon Gekko of journalism. Neuharth is a colorful fellow who enjoys indulging his eccentricities (he built a treehouse in his backyard where he does most of his "writing and thinking"). He also takes great pride in portraying himself as a hard guy who joyfully squashed all rivals on his unstoppable climb to power. This is a man who titled his autobiography *Confessions of an SOB*. To his credit, Neuharth granted uncensored space in it to his ex-wife. She wrote that Neuharth is "a snake."

Neuharth may be an SOB but he isn't stupid. He was shrewd enough to design a newspaper that did not reflect his unpleasant personality. In the case of *USA Today*, SOB stands for Sort of Bland. The paper projects a slick, upbeat, impersonal, superficial character. Politics aside, if *USA Today* were a person it would be Dan Quayle.

Despite his executive triumphs, Al Neuharth never forgot his origins as a working journalist. Every so often he got a yen to go out and cut through the viscous media blather and personally give *USA Today* readers the lowdown. This impulse led to the memorable JetCapade, a whirlwind tour of the globe in a specially outfitted plane in which The Founder and a handpicked team of reporters descended on one hapless nation after another and Neuharthized the poor inhabitants before they knew what had hit them.

It was a glorious quest. In a matter of only seven months, the JetCapaders had achieved their impossible dream: To thoroughly explain to *USA Today* readers everything of significance in the entire world.

Media Person was so impressed by the flow of profound insights emanating from the high-flying super-editor and his crack news team that he memorized entire passages. A typically unforgettable effort was the dispatch that began:

CAIRO, Egypt—The USA and the world have been intrigued or awe-inspired for hundreds of years by this seat of ancient civilization.

- Pyramids and the Sphinx.
- Limitless Saharan deserts and the lush Nile Valley.
- Camels and turban-wrapped peddlers and workers.

Unbelievable! They had done it again. In one swift laser ray of incisive prose, the JetCapaders had captured the essence of the Egyptian experience and its impact on mankind, while avoiding the clichés and superficialities of ordinary journalism.

Media Person remembers putting his *USA Today* aside, sighing deeply, and shaking his head in awed reverence. There was no reason to read further. Al Neuharth, that magnificent, incredible, globe-hopping SOB, had said it all.

The Rise of
the Editor Class

Crime Story used to be Media Person's favorite crime story until the week Jann Wenner showed up. On seeing the pudgy *Rolling Stone* editor/publisher, who was attempting to impersonate an actor, Media Person emitted a horrible scream of mingled fright and rage that must have startled the neighbors sitting just beyond the paper-thin wallboard that fails to separate New York apartments.

Here was yet another hideous magazine trend to send Media Person reeling in pain: editors becoming famous.

It wasn't right and it wasn't fair. The country was better off when editors were anonymous drudges wearing green eyeshades who were kept out of public view and allowed to inflict their tedious personalities only on journalists, who were used to abuse and could handle it. Old-style editors knew their job was enhancing the creations of writers, which required suppression of their own egos.

Celebrity editors? That's all wrong. It's writers who are supposed to get the few remaining fame slots assigned the literary world. They do the creative work. They make the sacrifices, opting for insecurity, neuroses, and less money. For their pain, most of them die obscure, depressed, and addicted to something expensive. Editors on the other hand get power and the immense satisfaction of constantly rejecting writers and making sure the payroll department loses their checks. For this, the price editors must pay is anonymity. That's the deal that was cut way back at the dawn of media.* But now, of course, no one wants to pay the price. Suppression is obsolete. Everyone wants everything.

So now we get glamorpuss editors. The Condé Nast fashion-magazine factory discovered a devastating weapon, the Brainy British Beauty, which it began importing in high volume. The two best known, Tina Brown of *Vanity Fair* and Anna Wintour of *Vogue*, lost little time infiltrating the American gossip columns and society circuit. Soon, not content with editing magazine articles, they *were* magazine articles. Everyone was writing about them.

Brown made the cover of *Newsweek*. Her pioneering innovation, a concept previously unknown in all journalistic history, was variety. *Okay, troops: We'll put a movie star on the cover but inside we'll print a piece on AIDS!* Gasps are gasped and several staffers faint dead away on hearing the startling strategy.

When Anna Wintour was named editor of the year by another magazine, *Adweek*, Condé Nast bought a self-congratulatory full-page ad in *The New York Times* that consisted of a photo of Wintour, dressed to kill and maim as well, twenty inches high. At one point the window of Barney's, a trendy New York clothing store, featured a mannequin modeled after her.

A new level of escalation began when Rupert Murdoch, the unstoppable Australian media swallower, started a new fashion magazine to compete with *Vogue*. He named it not *Fabulous Duds* or *Better Than Vogue* but *Mirabella*, after its editor, Grace Mirabella, who had been replaced at *Vogue* by Anna Wintour. So now Grace Mirabella was famous too.

---

*Between Johannes Gutenberg, inventor of the printing press, and Satan.

And now, on top of all that, the egregious Wenner was barging into the fantasy lives of poor, innocent, escapism-dependent TV viewers. What next, a magazine editor running for president?

If so, it would probably be Michael Kinsley, who stopped editing *The New Republic* so he could be a regular on the TV show *Crossfire* and spend his evenings scowling at Patrick Buchanan.

Watching Wenner, Media Person hoped that *Crime Story*'s Lieutenant Torello, the most brutal cop since Fearless Fosdick, might crush the interloper's face with one eloquent paw, as he often did with undesirables, then yell "Cuff the puke," and work in a cordovan wingtip to the rib cage as his beefy Chicago detectives dragged Wenner to the squad car, but as this prospect faded, Media Person sank gradually into sullen torpor and then a troubled sleep.

He never watched *Crime Story* again.

Why They Always Get It Wrong

Media Person loves the media. He is completely and utterly hooked on the media. The media is, or possibly are,* his entire life. After all, Media is his first name. Everything Media Person knows he learned from the media.

None of this, however, means that Media Person believes anything the media tell him.

Because for all their charms the media have a major flaw: They get everything wrong.

Most people have come to realize this, but they don't really understand why. They think there's some political conspiracy going on. They don't understand the real problem: It's impossible for human beings to get anything important right and communi-

---

*No one knows if the word is singular or plural anymore. It used to be purely plural but now it's in flux. This makes the writing of a book on media impossible. Media Person nearly gave up on several occasions. He finally decided that the word can be either singular or plural depending on how he feels at the moment and the hell with it.

cate it accurately to other human beings. The media are doomed to fail.

There are at least fourteen reasons for this and probably a few others Media Person could think of if he had the time. But this will do for a start:

1. *Frequency:* The news goes out too often. It's hard to find enough significant news to fill a monthly or weekly magazine, but, incredible as it may seem, there are newspapers and TV news shows that appear every day. Just trying to fill that gaping maw is exhausting, let alone getting the stuff right. This is why the media are so riddled with clichés, repetition, errors, and fluff. If a newspaper came out only when necessary, say four times a year, it would be superb. But then, of course, the owner couldn't make any money.

2. *Sheer Incompetence:* A problem in any area involving humans, a notoriously screwed-up species. Just as there are doctors who can't tell a spleen from a nostril and generals who inadvertently order their own troops shelled, there are editors who can't spell, reporters who can't get a fact straight, and delivery boys who toss the paper on the wrong porch. Even in smart, competent people, the human brain doesn't always work that well. There are memory failures, glitches, slips, and fatigue. You know Margaret Thatcher was prime minister of Britain but you type "Margaret O'Brien" and no editor catches it. An anchorman says, "We are at war," when he means, "That's the news, good night." Happens all the time.

3. *Laziness:* Another human-problem area of major proportions, one with which Media Person himself is more than a little familiar. Reporting takes enormous energy and stamina. A reporter may have to make thirty-six phone calls or pore over a thousand-page document written entirely in legalese to nail down one elusive fact. He may have to badger, cajole, whine, and wheedle to get sources to open their mouths. He may have to do all this for months or even years. Sometimes it's tempting to knock off for the day instead of knocking on those last dozen doors.

4. *Bias:* Political, national, religious, tribal, regional, cultural, class, ethnic, racial, age, gender, height; you name it and some benighted human has it and will be powerless to prevent it from seeping into his—oops, sorry—or her copy.

5. *Deadlines:* Journalism's built-in bar to completeness. A historian may take ten years to research the complex story that a newspaper or TV reporter worked on forty-seven minutes before the boss started screaming, "Time's up. Go with what you got!"

6. *The Slippery Nature of Reality:* It's a deceptively difficult subject to master, reality, elusive and complex. Even if you knew every relevant fact about a big unfolding story such as Watergate, it still wouldn't be easy to explain clearly. And usually you're missing many of the facts.

7. *Newness:* The nature of news, by definition, contains a lot of material that is *new*. Being new, the stuff is unfamiliar, strange, and thus hard to believe, let alone understand, the first time you encounter it. Humans are much better at grasping things they've heard many times before. Think about the rise of AIDS and how difficult it was for people to separate facts from rumors as this frightening disease advanced.

8. *Absence:* When news happens, reporters are not always on the scene. Crimes, for instance, usually are committed without the press being alerted. Earthquakes do not send out press releases. The really interesting political developments occur behind closed doors. The reporters show up afterward and have to play catch-up and piece things together secondhand. It's hard enough to figure out what happened if you saw it happen, let alone reconstruct it later. And it's even harder when a reporter must face . . .

9. *Noncooperation:* Often the people who know what's really going on don't want the public to know what's really going on. Or they fear the media won't see their side of it. So they avoid the media or lie to it.

10. *Process:* Routine, everyday newsroom operations ensure screw-ups. A reporter goes on vacation and his replacement doesn't know the beat. A story goes through three editors and one of them scribbles in what he thinks is an improvement but is really

an error. Static on the line makes a rewriteman think the reporter said "gun" when she said "bun." A printer drops the word "not," reversing the meaning of the sentence. The possibilities are endless.

11. *Fear:* Sometimes journalists are reluctant to go after a powerful individual or organization for fear of reprisals. Sometimes they fear the economic consequences of offending big advertisers or large groups of readers. Sometimes the journalists are not afraid but their bosses are, which brings us to

12. *Meddling Bosses:* Publishers, owners, and TV executives sometimes interfere with the news in ways large and small. They may suppress stories harmful to their business interests or those of their political allies or advertisers. They may insist on an upbeat worldview even when the world is going to pot. They may drive reporters crazy with irrational rules. Ted Turner, the founder and owner of CNN, banned the word *foreign* when he decided that it had a pejorative ring and would not speed the advent of brotherhood among nations. This caused (according to a story that may be apocryphal but is too good to resist) a sportscaster on Turner's TBS to say that a ballgame was briefly delayed because the batter had an international object in his eye.

13. *Footprints:* Human beings have an unfortunate need to invest a part of themselves in everything they do. If they tell a story, they want to put their own spin on it. This tendency requires a reporter to make her story just a little more interesting, more dramatic, more important, more vital. To make it her own. And it requires an editor to add something, anything. To make his contribution. They simply can't help themselves.

14. *House Style:* Most publications and broadcasts have a prescribed style of communicating. It is drilled into newcomers through instruction and example. And often it is limiting. Like it or not, tabloid reporters must write simple, short, punchy sentences that discourage complexity and subtlety. Many publications require a detached, impersonal, semiformal prose—called objectivity—that makes it difficult or even impossible for reporters to impart certain experiences or observations. Rare is the reporter who has not found himself in a bar after work telling friends in his

natural mode of expression all the things that had to be left out of the story—i.e., the best parts.

What all this is leading up to is Media Person's First (and Only) Rule of Media Watching: Be skeptical.

Accept nothing on faith. Trust no one (except Media Person when he tells you to trust no one). Laugh in the anchorman's face. Scoff at headlines. Consider all information false until proven otherwise. And then accept it only slowly and grudgingly. Read forty-six newspapers every day so you don't depend on one fallible source.

Follow this simple rule, as Media Person does, and you will never end up drowning in a flash flood because you confidently sashayed out in the street after reading in the papers that the severe dry spell in your area would continue unabated for the next three weeks.

True, your daily horoscope will no longer be the perfect guide to life it once was, but your chance of surviving the day will dramatically improve.

The Phantom
of Oprah

If you could have your entire body removed from the neck down and replaced by that of any celebrity, whose would you choose?

This is the kind of question Media Person thinks about frequently in the Posthistoric Era, which we are now inhabiting, according to a *New York Times* article he read. In the Posthistoric Era, all the big questions have been answered, our fabulous liberal democratic capitalist system (invented by Alexander Hamilton and perfected by Neil Bush) has prevailed over all other politico-economic models, the great upheavals of history have all been heaved up and there can be no more world wars, great adventures, conquering heroes, profound revolutions, or new, world-shaking ideologies that inspire millions before killing them. In fact, there's really nothing to do now but a little fine tuning of the existing system and, for those of philosophical bent, some grappling with the small questions—sometimes *very* small.

Such as whether it is ethical to snatch Ann-Margret's body and glue the living head of Oprah Winfrey on top of it.

While science cannot yet accomplish such a deed, media can.

And *TV Guide* did. Its editors considered Oprah's face to have excellent sales potential but had their doubts about the rest of her. So, unbeknown to either woman (or its readers) the magazine employed the able-bodied Ann-Margret to portray Lower Oprah on the cover.

This must have been a dismaying turn of events for the extroverted talk-show mogul. Oprah had just publicly dieted off vast amounts of lard using secret potions passed down from one celebrity to another over the ages, and yet her sleek new Oprah bod still wasn't sexy enough to meet the exacting standards set by *TV Guide* under its new boss, Rupert Murdoch, owner of every media property in America not owned by Ted Turner. (Imagine how ashamed Media Person was to think that he had once worried that Murdoch would cheapen and debase the magazine.)

But what no one seemed to notice in the uproar following revelation of the wondrous operation was the fact that it marked the leap from television to print of the exciting new trend of reenactment.

Reenactment had caused a stir when TV news shows began using actors to stage news events. Critics—the kind of critics who start grousing every time broadcast journalists try to have any fun at all—said there was something wrong with putting a bunch of actors on the screen and calling that news. It was really show biz, they whined, and there is supposed to be a difference.

But *TV Guide*'s story on Oprah Winfrey was news *about* show biz, so in the minds of its editors, a little recasting probably seemed less than a major sin.

In fact, it could be argued, *TV Guide* was pioneering a new hyperreality. This was better than plain, mundane old truth because it gave readers a kind of super-Oprah who was sexier and more glamorous than the actual Oprah. Ann-Oprah was probably what Oprah herself would have liked to look like if she'd been able to manage it.

TV Guide had blazed a path through this confusing posthistoric, postjournalistic era we live in—an era in which all news stories have already been written, leaving humanity with the awful prospect of facing only endless repetition of the same old stories, with minor variations.

Obviously there was only one solution to the fatal boredom and paralysis that leads to: Making stuff up.

TV Guide made up a brand-new hybrid celebrity. Some call it fake. Some call it sleazy, dishonest pandering. Media Person calls it journalism at its creative best.

Ad Nauseam

Media Person gives up.

Media Person can no longer resist the greatest force of our age. Not democracy, not capitalism, certainly not any religion or scientific discovery. It's advertising.

The question is not whether advertising is good or bad but how to get away from it long enough to catch one breath without someone trying to sell you something. Advertising has taken over all human life and will not rest till it finds a way to take over death, too.

There used to be limits, havens from the tide of meretricious swill engulfing us. But now advertising has invaded nearly all of them. Consider:

Lawyers, doctors, and dentists now advertise.

The armed forces advertise.

There is advertising in hardcover books.

There is advertising in outer space: In September 1989, the Soviets launched a Soyuz TM-8 capsule on a booster rocket emblazoned with an ad for the Italian insurance company Generali.

Dial the phone number that gives you time or weather and first you hear a commercial.

Go to the movies and you get commercials before the feature film. Then you get secret commercials *in* the feature film itself in the form of ever more intrusive product placements. After the movie you find on sale toys, T-shirts, books, and souvenirs and realize that the film itself was nothing but a commercial for all the products being spun off it.

There are commercials on movie videos and cable TV, which originally were supposed to be a refuge from commercials.

Religions now make TV commercials. And the Catholic Church hired a public-relations firm (PR is a slightly more subtle and insidious form of advertising) to promote its stand against abortion.

TV advertising dominates elections and, not uncoincidentally, politics has become little more than empty slogans and sound bites. Controversy is avoided, substance is avoided, reality is avoided.

Political *issues* have become advertising vehicles. Corporations looking for an edge attach their name to fighting drugs or cleaning up the environment, anything that will score points with the public and give the company a concerned, caring image.

Many of the new magazines born in the '70s and '80s are basically marketing concepts rather than editorial concepts—primarily vehicles to deliver readers to advertisers.

In magazines are more and more "advertorials," ads cleverly disguised to fool readers into thinking they're reading editorial matter.

Advertisers put corporate emblems on the clothing of golfers and the outsides of race cars. Ads fly over cities on blimps and hot-air balloons. They decorate the walls of athletic stadiums. In some sports arenas, the team bench has been pushed behind the goal so the players will not obscure the billboards along the sidelines. The rhythms of baseball and football have been altered to suit the needs of commercials.

Labels, which used to be on the inside of clothing, are now often on the outside, a form of free advertising.

There is no longer any shame in selling your name. George Plimpton, the respected editor and writer, posed for an ad for tuxedos. Tip O'Neill, the former speaker of the House, did so many commercials he became a living billboard. Five Chicago aldermen appeared in an ice-cream commercial. In the fifteenth season of *Saturday Night Live,* the satirical show once known for its parodies of commercials, most of the cast began working as pitchmen in real commercials.

Stars the ad agencies can't buy, they steal. They'll shamelessly appropriate the identity, voice, or likeness of a dead star for a commercial. Sometimes a living one, too.

You can't even find rest in the restroom: An ad agency in Knoxville, Tennessee, places ads above the urinals and inside the toilet stalls of public lavatories.

And that is why Media Person wants you to drink Löwenbräu and smoke Marlboros. Media Person implores you to eat Starkist tuna and subscribe to *Time* and drive a Honda. Media Person is endorsing everything he can think of. He is selling out big.

This chapter is brought to you by Sony. Buy a new cassette for your Walkman and hum along to this book. To keep the book clean, wash it with Tide, along with your Calvin Klein jeans and your Nike sneakers. Eat Big Macs till you puke. Swig some Pepto-Bismol and you'll feel better fast. Then you can start your Ultra-Slim Fast diet. Media Person does all of the above and he's lost forty pounds in the last three chapters and his breath is fresher, too, because he gargles with Listerine. Buy the large economy size now or he'll kill you.

What single incident finally caused Media Person to snap he isn't sure.

Maybe it was the dog-food ad in *Life*, the most revolting Media Person has ever seen. Apparently aimed at affluent dogs ("Special Pet Foods Found Only at Special Places") the ad included a color illustration of "stool," as it was termed in the copy. A spot quiz advised dog owners to examine their pets' "stool size and consistency" and note whether the specimens are:

A. Small and firm. 30 pts.
B. Large and hard. 5 pts.
C. Large and very soft. 0 pts.

Henry Luce must have been peeing in his grave.

Or maybe it was the *National Geographic*'s hundredth birthday. The high-class, high-integrity *National Geographic* went cosmic on Media Person with an eerie, shimmering, silvery 3-D globe on its cover that symbolized the fragility of the planet. That was fine. It was the back cover that stunned Media Person. It contained an eerie, shimmering, silvery 3-D *McDonald's restaurant*. Media Person figured maybe this symbolized the fragility of the human stomach. Had *National Geographic* slipped off its axis? Did the staff lick some hallucinogenic toadstools on its last slog through the Amazon? Or did it just succumb to the greatest force of our age?

Maybe it was Christopher Whittle* striving to sell a specially made TV news show—one full of commercials—to be shown regularly in America's public schools.

Maybe it was the ad where a red-bearded man fondly gazes at a glass of beer and says: "Guinness Gold. If only my father had lived to see it." Boy, there's a real sentimentalist. Talk about family values. This guy imagines the negation of his father's death—and to what end? Does he want Dad to see Sis's new baby or hear about Junior winning the scholarship to medical school or Granny getting over her hiatal hernia? No, the most pressing reason he can come up with to justify the greatest miracle since Lazarus is to hand dear Dad *a beer.*

Hey, Pop, wait till you try these suds—then you can jump happily back into your hole and croak for good.

Maybe it was Reebok using pro basketball stars to pitch a new sneaker you have to pump up with air before wearing—a product with no real reason for being—except to sucker ghetto kids into forking over about $150.

---

*Christopher Whittle, the most dangerous man in America, whose Whittle Communications specializes in dreaming up ways to insert advertising in hitherto virgin territory, makes a terrifying return visit to *Read My Clips* on page 108. Those with weak hearts are advised to skip it.

Maybe it was Romania. According to an article in *The Wall Street Journal*, the poor Romanians for some time had been using Kent cigarettes for money, due to the worthlessness of the official currency. "The value of Kents is watched in Romania the way currency fluctuations are followed in other countries," the *Journal* reported.

Kent's advertising people lost little time turning the article into a full-page ad in papers like *USA Today*. "In Romania, Kents are too valuable to smoke," went the headline. "Fortunately, we live in America."

Where we get to have all the cancer we want— Is this a great country or what?

It occurred to Media Person that he was witnessing a first. Of course commercials have long cajoled tourists to vacation in beautiful Haiti or Beirut, but this was different. Romania had become— albeit inadvertently—the first celebrity spokescountry.

"Hi, we're Romania, and we smoke Kents. Try 'em—or you're under arrest."

Maybe it was the debut of McDonald's in Moscow, an event that got more free publicity than the Russian revolution. Those poor clucks, Media Person thought, swept in one stroke from communist oppression to capitalist cholesterol contamination. McDonald's was the most effective advertiser to jump on the de-communization bandwagon but hardly the only one. Admen immediately adjust to any change and co-opt it. A New York store called ABC Warehouse Outlet ran newspaper ads headlined:

A SALE THAT DEALS THE FINAL BLOW TO COMMUNISM.
CAPITALISM AT ITS BEST. EVERYTHING IS INEXPENSIVE.

Not long after that Media Person saw a computer ad that tried to put the whole global struggle for freedom in perspective:

FIRST, THEY TEAR DOWN THE BERLIN WALL. THEN, THEY
LOWER THE PRICE OF THE MACINTOSH SE. WHAT A GREAT TIME
TO BE A HUMAN BEING.

General Electric did an extraordinary TV commercial after communism died in Hungary. You saw a flock of wonderful-looking old-world Europeans in evening dress waltzing around a baroque opera house, above them a spectacular chandelier bursting into brilliant light, symbolizing their newly won liberty. The GE connection was a contract the company had signed with the Hungarians to go into the electricity business there, but the implication was that somehow it was General Electric making possible this whole new era of freedom. Watching the Hungarians speak with tears in their eyes of their happiness and their hopes for tomorrow, Media Person found himself nearly weeping and yet, oddly enough, at the same time felt his lunch coming up as another part of him recoiled violently at being taken in even briefly by this shameless manipulation.

Maybe it was one of those ads that made Media Person lose it.

Or maybe it was the day he saw the Ultimate Endorsement. Yes, that was it. Media Person remembers now. That was when he finally snapped. That was when he got religion and decided to go forth and plug. He was either having a vision or sleeping—hard to be sure which—but suddenly, there was God on His Throne, and for some reason, He was doing the Creation all over again. "Let there be light," God thundered and instantly a radiant glow transformed the vast empty darkness. Then a magnificent new planet came into being, our beloved Earth, now shining brightly in the first morning dew, waiting to be stocked with billions of freshly minted living organisms.

But something was wrong. The Supreme Ruler was frowning. Thunder was heard. Media Person trembled when he saw how wrathful was the Lord.

"No, no, no," God raged till the very heavens shook. "I wanted a *Bud Lite*."

I Read the News Today, Oh Boy

Lord, the things you read. How does Media Person stand it? He has only one defense. He talks back to the press. That's right. Just opens his mouth and blurts whatever rude sarcasm comes to mind. Psychologists say this is excellent for your mental health and Media Person recommends it highly. Of course, your relatives or colleagues may find you strange, sitting there sneering and telling off the newspaper. This is why Media Person lives alone.

Try it yourself and see how healthy you feel. Here are a few historic examples to get you started.

Media Person read in *The New York Times*: "Gen. Juan D. Perón died in 1974, but his ghost continues to wander the corridors of power in Argentina."

And we thought we had problems here with Elvis.

He read in *USA Today*: "Close political advisers Craig Fuller and Robert Teeter, who literally hovered at Bush's elbow throughout the campaign . . ."

No wonder Bush won the election. Dukakis made his people obey the law of gravity.

In an *Esquire* story on the paternalistic *Los Angeles Times*: "It takes care of its employees from cradle to grave."

You really have to hand it to an outfit that can spot talent that young.

From a Hollywood gossip column by Marilyn Beck: "[Sylvester Stallone] reportedly absorbs more devastatingly brutal beatings, trashings and psychological head-bashings than he has in all 14 of his other films combined. One wonders how long he can take such punishment."

One also wonders how long Marilyn Beck has been covering Hollywood without anyone telling her that movie actors pull their punches, not to mention using stunt doubles.

And what the hell is psychological head-bashing? Someone bops Sly with Dr. Joyce Brothers?

From the *New York Post*: "Bush is a 'phonaholic' who calls everyone in sight."

If they're in sight, why does he need the phone?

From *New York Newsday*: "Prostate cancer is by no means a trivial disease."

Gee, Media Person always thought you just pop a couple of aspirin and knock it right out.

From the *Post*: "Kid from Bronx to Become Nation's Top General."

Well, if Quayle became vice president, anything's possible.

From the *Times*: "A leper doesn't change its spots."

No and a rhinoplasty can be dangerous if he charges you in open country.

From *New York Newsday*: "Rose's Hearing Blocked."

Poor Pete. First that gambling mess, now excess earwax.

From the *Post*: "Maybe this is what William Churchill meant by '*The Gathering Storm*.' "

Or maybe it's what Winston Shakespeare meant by *The Tempest*. Who knows?

From the *Times*: "College courses on the Vietnam war have exploded in the last few years."

Those damn Vietcong never know when to stop.

From the cover of *Lear's*: "Babies Over 40."

Must be hell on the parents having to get up in the middle of the night to bring the crying kid his Alka-Seltzer.

From the *Post*: "Hunters Stand Behind Bush."

Sure, it may look funny to some but when an enraged bull rabbit is on the loose, a man needs every trick he can find.

From *USA Today*: "Some scientists say they're getting closer to the causes of chronic fatigue syndrome.

"But despite progress, experts converging on San Francisco for the first national forum on the issue say the mysteries of CFS are far from being solved."

In other words, nothing's new but we've got a reporter at the meeting and lots of space to fill.

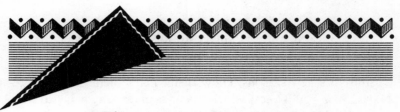

Sweepstime Is Icumen In

Some things never change, though offhand Media Person can't think of any.

Nowadays, most things do. Take the four seasons. Aeon after aeon, they rolled around, usually in the same order,* eternal and immutable. Or so we thought.

No more. Turned out the seasons were charming but obsolete. Take fall, for instance. Who has time anymore to notice whether the leaves have fallen off the trees or, given the depredations of pollution and the timber industry, whether there are any trees still standing? Fall was no longer relevant so it was quietly sacked, along with its three outmoded colleagues.

Today the rhythm of our lives is dictated by the media. And so are the new seasons we live by. There are five now because life is more complicated:

Fall Preview
Sweepstime

*Summer, Fall, Winter, Spring. (Source: *Encyclopaedia Britannica*)

Happy Holidays
Silly Season
Rerun

Study the new seasons, know them, mark them in your date-books. Soon you'll know which season is under way, what to wear in it, which fresh fruits and TV shows are available, and, most important, how to survive till the next season.

FALL PREVIEW

One day you are sluggish and torpid, your blood thick, your head groggy. You can barely move. Suddenly, all is different. There's a crackle in the air, a cool breeze. Your pulse quickens. Music is everywhere, a hot conga beat. Fashions change. Skirt hems rise, hair lengthens, pastels are out, tweed in. Wham! Sixteen thousand magazines and newspapers hit the newsstands fat and bursting with the word that all is new and fun again.

Fall Preview time is here.

This is the true New Year, the time of rebirth and renaissance. To find out what to do and how to live, you buy any magazine with an annual Fall Preview Issue (all of them) and you are thrilled to find that life is a carnival of wonderful new movies and plays and books. Television, at last free of reruns, will carry hilarious new sitcoms and thrilling dramatic series that are nothing like last year's stale, boring, cliché-ridden shows. Clothes will now be smart and flattering and beautiful. Brand-new foods are here, delicious but nonfattening.

And the business sector gets to advertise its products in a super-charged, superexcited media environment conducive to consumption frenzy. What a happy, busy time for all.

SWEEPSTIME

Sweepstime is unique: It's the only season that comes three times a year (November, February, and May). But you never need a calendar to know when it arrives. Before Sweepstime you're looking for a movie on TV and your choice is something like this:

Channel 2: *Friday the 13th Part XVIII*
Channel 4: *Hamburger—The Motion Picture*
Channel 6: *Nancy Drew and the Hidden Broccoli*

Next day you look again. This time you see:

Channel 2: *All About Eve*
Channel 4: *The Manchurian Candidate*
Channel 6: Double Feature—*Citizen Kane* and *Raiders of the Lost Ark*.

Yep, it's Sweepstime.

What we need in the U.S., Media Person has always felt, is a TV movie czar, an official government regulator with dictatorial powers, who ensures that good movies are evenly spread over the tube. But until that happens, we must take what bounty Sweepstime offers, set our VCRs, and gorge.

And what bounty there is. Not only are there great movies at Sweepstime, there are also miniseries and specials. And the news and talk shows are full of hilarious trash. Sex in the Mafia! Lesbian Vampires on Drugs! Phil and Geraldo take on Oprah in Mud-Wrestling!

Interestingly this merry season is founded on a completely irrational principle. During Sweepstime, the ratings companies measure viewing patterns to determine advertising rates. But knowing this, all the channels schedule special programming during the period. As a result, the ratings don't reflect normal viewing habits so they are meaningless. Thus Sweepstime is a colossal fraud.

But so what? Let's enjoy it while we can. Revel in the short burst of quality. At Sweepstime, there's no need to leave home. Settle in before the screen, let the pleasant torpor of sweet Sweepstime creep over you, and by the time you regain consciousness it may well be . . .

HAPPY HOLIDAYS

Just as our seasons have changed, so have our holidays. Christmas began as a religious observance and evolved into a celebration of shopping. Thanksgiving, originating as an occasion of gratitude to the Divinity for a bountiful harvest, became an orgy of gluttony topped off by football. On Independence Day, formerly a patriotic celebration, half the populace cowers indoors as the other half discharges firearms into the air. Easter has something to do with rabbits and eggs. For most people, Memorial Day and Labor Day mean going to the beach.

But all of those have faded in importance. Today America's most important holidays are Oscar Day, Super Bowl Sunday, the Miss America Pageant, Presidential Election Day, Earth Day, Tax Deadline Day, and World Series Week. And then there is our longest celebration. It began as a cluster of nearly forgotten individual holidays that have now been incorporated into a nearly endless festive season collectively known as Happy Holidays.

This season lasts for nearly three months, during which Americans do progressively less work and more partying. It begins somewhere between Halloween (a once-charming night of fantasy for children appropriated by teenage vandals and drag queens) and Thanksgiving and runs through Christmas and New Year's, winding down slightly as it approaches its climax, Super Bowl Sunday, when the entire populace gathers before its TV screens to watch beer commercials and eat junk food.

The ancient New Year's holiday, incidentally, has given way to something called the Year-End Wrap-up. Even though the year really begins at Fall Preview time, all the media now pretend otherwise and deliver themselves of endless summaries, predictions, and joky fictional awards such as *Esquire*'s annual Dubious Achievements, which berate those who have erred, failed, or made fools of themselves and are considered safe targets for ridicule.

In the main, Happy Holidays celebrate the modern American values: shopping, partying, sports watching, overconsumption, random excess, and the production of really big hangovers.

SILLY SEASON

Silly Season begins immediately after Super Bowl Sunday and continues until it peters out into sullen depression. During Silly Season, the media fill up with fakery, flackery, quackery, hoaxes, and humbug. This is because all the frantic celebrating of Happy Holidays leaves people exhausted and vulnerable. They quickly fall victim to flu, flimflams, fluff, folderol, flummoxery, and worst of all, alliteration.

In New York, the onset of Silly Season is marked by the ancient tabloid ritual of the Polar Bear Club. Photos mysteriously appear of flaccid old people who, for reasons never made clear—perhaps an impulse to emulate the lemming, perhaps a desperate need to show off bad bodies—lope into the freezing sea at Coney Island. Many turn blue and drop dead but the newspapers never report this as it would mar the festive nature of the pseudoevent. Ancient newspaper rules mandate that the headline above the photo of the grinning fatties in the surf must be a bad pun. Anything stupid will do, though most editors insist on either

POLAR BRRRS!

or

GRIN AND BEAR IT!

In Silly Season, atmospheric changes stimulate the hormones of the nation's public-relations people, or flacks, rousing them to frantic activity. The news desks of America are soon awash in inane press releases of no conceivable interest to anyone. Most are quickly printed or aired.

Attention-starved hucksters fronting nonexistent organizations announce fictional polls and phony awards. Zsa Zsa Gabor is chosen "the year's top whiner" on "National Whiners' Day" and "Man Watchers, Inc." names "The Year's Most Watchable People" and someone calling himself "Mr. Blackwell" hypes his predictably petulant "worst-dressed list." These and other absurdities are presented to the public as news. Anyone wishing to discuss anything of importance must wait till the end of Silly Season.

RERUN

An unbearably hot, bleak season which taxes everyone's patience, Rerun seems to get longer every year. People are bored and short-tempered. There is nothing to do. You've seen everything on TV and the newspapers and magazines are anorexic because advertising dries up. The murder rate rises. So do drug and alcohol consumption. Neighbor turns against neighbor and nations feel like nuking the country next door. If not for video rentals, many Americans would not survive this terrible time. It is vital to drink as many fluids as possible, take constant showers, and conserve your energy with lengthy naps. Remember: The more you sleep the more likely you are to survive ruinous Rerun.

'Twas Ratings Killed the Beast

In theory, Media Person approved of *Beauty and the Beast* but was never able to work himself into a romantic enough state to join the cult of believers and attempt actual viewing.

B & B was about a creature who looked not unlike the Cowardly Lion from *The Wizard of Oz*, inhabited a shadowy subterranean world beneath New York City, and hung out with a beautiful assistant district attorney. He was sort of The Phantom of the Sewer System.

From reading analyses of the show in academic journals and *TV Guide*, Media Person gathered that it appealed mainly to women. They found in Vincent, the extremely sensitive feline hero, their idealized, impossible, unfulfilled vision of the perfect man: i.e., a guy who would actually listen to them. Not only would he listen, he would understand them and eagerly discuss the awful, controversial subject that living men will have nothing to do with: feelings.

Perhaps the reason the show was eventually canceled was that America could only handle one Phil Donahue at a time.

Or perhaps people finally became bored with the ever-hanging question of whether Vincent and Catherine, his human friend, would remain platonic soulmates or attempt prime-time interspecies coitus.

It was a question that caused the producers much anxiety and soul-searching. Still in doubt as the climactic—so to speak—episode approached, they prepared two different endings. In one, the couple would share their first tender, romantic kiss. In the second version, more explicit but reportedly just as emotional, Vincent would rub up against Catherine's ankle and she would scratch behind his ears.*

*Media Person includes this regrettable paragraph only as a historic example of the kind of joke being done at the time by every TV comedian in America. In the 1988–89 era, only Vice President Dan Quayle was the butt of more late-night television jokes than Vincent. At least Media Person's Vincent joke didn't involve a litter box, like most of Johnny Carson's. After *Beauty and the Beast* was canceled, either Jay Leno or David Letterman—or maybe both—said that Vincent was joining the cast of *Dynasty* as a fur coat.

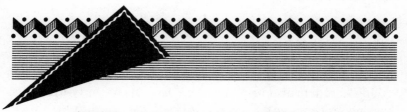

There's No Bits
Like Obits

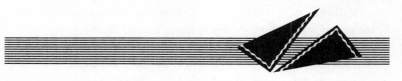

According to obituary notices, a mean and useless citizen never dies.
—CLARENCE DARROW

Like cemeteries, obituaries discriminate.

Just as they get bigger tombs, the rich, powerful, and famous get bigger obits. So do people who work for the newspaper—and their relatives. If you want a four-column headline celebrating your death, your best bet is to have a son and steer him toward a career as a printer or pressman. (It also helps to die on a slow news day.)

Few presidents, kings, or Nobel Prize winners ever got as nice a sendoff from *The New York Times* as the world-famous Iphigene Sulzberger. What? You never heard of Iphigene? Hers was a voluminous obit, starting on page one, next to a huge, flattering twenty-nine-year-old photo, and jumping to the back where it roamed vast acreage.

The obit lovingly recounted the vital role Mrs. Sulzberger had played in the protracted, far-flung searches that were held whenever the *Times* required new publishers, three of whom, by an odd coincidence, turned out to have been her husband, son, and son-in-law.

Which served to reconfirm the ancient wisdom of Mel Brooks: It's good to be queen.

Quirks of fate also help. You may have spent thirty-five years bagging groceries at the A&P, but if you happened to have been a passenger on the *Titanic* you are guaranteed a prominent obit. *Titanic* survivors always make the obit page.

Many obits are dull. For weeks it can seem like only uninteresting people are allowed to die. But then you fall into a bonanza of weird trivia. On May 31, 1990, for instance, readers of the *Times* were rewarded with two short but fascinating obits. There was Edward Louie, inventor of the fortune-cookie folding machine, and Millicent Miller, who was Vivien Leigh's stand-in in *Gone With the Wind*. Or, more accurately, her hand-in.

"It was her hand," said the obit, "that pulled a turnip from the ground after the ruination of Scarlett's plantation Tara, and it was her hand drawing a revolver from a drawer before Scarlett shot a Union soldier."

Obits tend to be circumspect affairs. As Clarence Darrow knew, it is considered bad form to say anything negative about the deceased. Euphemisms and omissions are the rule. As a result, obits are a good indication of societal taboos and fears. Sometimes what's left out is more interesting than what's put in. Obit buffs live between the lines.

For a long time, cancer could not be mentioned and so people were constantly dying of lengthy or lingering illnesses. AIDS now carries a similar stigma, but that disease became more mentionable after gay groups campaigned to get newspapers to say it out loud; they wanted the extent of the epidemic known.

AIDS also reformed another obit-page tradition, the listing of survivors. This custom had been a great annoyance to Media Person long before the AIDS era, because of the absurd inaccuracy of a stock phrase long used in obits:

Mr. Footlick is survived by his wife, Miranda, a brother, Ludwig, of the Cameroons, and two grandchildren.

This always makes Media Person want to grab a pencil and add: *and approximately six billion other people*.

AIDS activists have brought about only a small expansion of the survivor list, but at least it's a step forward. Now, on many papers, not only relatives are acceptable: Someone known as a "longtime companion" may be listed. That is, a lover.

Of course, for an obit to say that the deceased also had a strong relationship with a mistress or a pet schnauzer or a favorite TV show or a detested enemy would be too interesting, too real, too far outside the bounds of sterile formula writing and minimal reportage that rules the obit page.

What it comes down to, finally, is that if you want a really good obit, you can't trust the local newspaper. You have to write it yourself.

Remember, your obit is the final summing up of your entire life. It is usually the last thing people read about you (and in some cases, the first). Thus it may well determine humanity's opinion of you *for the rest of eternity*.

Can you afford to leave something that important in the hands of the distracted, overworked strangers who typically inhabit the newsroom, many of whom cannot even be counted on to spell your name correctly?

Of course not. That is why Media Person is going to help you to compose your own obit. Don't worry. It won't take long. After you're dead, you'll be glad you did it.

When we're finished, you'll give the obit to the executor of your will with instructions to send copies to the local newspapers and wire services as soon as you expire or even look ill. No sense in taking chances.

Even if the newspaper should edit or rewrite you, it will give you a better shake. Because the less work you cause newspaper people, the more they like you.

Let's begin.

The most important part of an obit is the lead, or first paragraph. Though it can be short, it must contain four compulsory elements:

1. *Your name:* This helps the reader differentiate you from the other dead people on the page.

2. *The fact that you died:* Even though everyone on the obit page is dead, newspaper editors have learned never to assume too much intelligence on the part of the readers, many of whom are themselves more dead than alive.

3. *Your age:* The single most important fact in any obit and the first one people read. If you're older than the reader, he'll feel reassured, taking it as evidence that death comes only to really ancient people. If younger, he'll gloat. *Ha! Another son of a bitch I outlasted!*

4. *Your major accomplishment:* This carefully chosen detail allows you to put your best foot forward and also answers a basic question that forms in the reader's mind after reading your name: "Who?" Of course it can be a problem for those who have no major accomplishments. The key rule here is to accentuate the positive. For example, say you are General Custer. There's an arrow in your kidney and war whoops all around; you sense your time is near, but you have a moment to dash off your obit lead.

Keep it positive. A person burdened by low self-esteem or excessive honesty might, under time pressure, produce the first lead below. That would be a mistake.

Wrong: General George Armstrong Custer, reckless and egomaniacal cavalry commander, was wiped out with his entire troop yesterday when he blundered into an obvious trap on the Little Big Horn.

Right: General George Armstrong Custer, 37, heavily decorated military hero who won numerous battles in the Civil War and Indian campaigns, died yesterday in valorous combat against numerically superior enemy forces.

What an improvement! And how about the rest of the obit?

Once you have your lead, the rest is a snap.

What Fugu These Morsels Be

One of the deepest impulses of our species is to inform a fellow human being that his act stinks.

That is why we have critics. Some people criticize critics and question whether they are necessary. Of course they aren't, but neither, strictly speaking, are people.

Media Person has always felt that critics would be more popular if they cultivated a measure of ambivalence. Why must they always be so damned sure of themselves? It smacks of raving arrogance. Just once, Media Person would like to read a review that said:

Well, I don't know what to tell you. While watching the film, I loved it. But then walking out of the theater, I overheard a woman say to her husband, "The plot really made no sense at all," and I suddenly realized, "Hey, she's right." On the other hand, the acting was very good—I *think*. I mean when you come right down to it, what *is* good acting, anyway? So now I'm not really sure at all.

Or this:

Remember yesterday when I wrote that *Jews on Horseback* was the worst movie ever made? Well, I realized the problem was I was in a terrible mood on account of my daughter running away with the census taker and now the more I think about it, the more that movie grows on me.

Media Person himself is probably too dependent on critics. He tries never to miss the film reviews of Gene Shalit and Joel "I Had a Wonderful Time! You're Gonna Love It!" Siegel. Whenever they praise a movie, Media Person goes out of his way to avoid it and has consequently missed millions of bad movies, or would have, except that then he accidentally runs across them on HBO at 2 A.M. and becomes inextricably involved before he knows it and can't stop watching and hates himself for it.

So much bad stuff is produced today, Media Person would rather read reviews than actually see the thing itself. At least the reviews are shorter. Sometimes he even writes reviews without seeing the thing itself.

A new Neil Simon play once opened on Broadway and Media Person immediately denounced it as artificial and forced. Too many tired gags and no sense of real danger to underpin the comic artifice.

Now traditionalists carped that Media Person shouldn't issue a verdict without seeing the play. But Media Person needs to have a strong opinion on everything. If you don't, no one respects you. But who has the time or energy to see everything? He had no choice.

It wasn't as if Media Person were totally ignorant of the Simon work. He caught a clip of it on TV news and saw all these noisy, self-adoring actors yelling and spitting and waving their arms. It was appalling. Media Person could have made his decision right there. But that would have been irresponsible.

Just because pols campaign in ten-second sound bites, people picket movies they haven't seen, and *USA Today* takes an inch to tell a story that fills two feet in *The New York Times*—that doesn't mean Media Person will compromise his high standards and form an opinion based on one clip.

So before issuing his critique, he waited till he'd read the newspapers. The critics all confirmed Media Person's instinct. Except for one, who was obviously a fool.

It was only then that Media Person allowed himself to issue his judgment. It is standing up quite nicely to the test of time, by the way.

All sorts of odd things are reviewed today but not all types of critics enjoy high esteem in Media Person's eyes. A few years ago during the notorious fugu scandal, he lost his taste for food critics.

Fugu is a puffer fish with a delicate taste so adored by Japanese gourmets that nothing stops them from eating it—not even the possibility that it may be their last meal. Improperly prepared, fugu has quite a kick. Its organs produce tetrodotoxin, a poison so lethal that even a small nibble can cause an embarrassing thud at a dinner party. So fugu is prepared only by experts carefully trained to recognize and remove the poison. Despite that, fugucide still claims one hundred Japanese gourmets a year.*

When the delectable death nosh first arrived in New York restaurants, Media Person eagerly read the numerous feature articles on it and quickly noticed something missing. Where were the eyewitness or, more accurately, mouthwitness accounts of fugu ingestion by our passionate restaurant critics?

There was only a scandalous silence. Media Person detected the rancid aroma of fugu fear. To chew or to eschew, that was the question. And the critics had shirked their duty, just because of a little risk of excruciatingly painful death. It was disgusting. These critics have a sacred trust. They are our stomachs, but it turned out they have no guts.

Besides, a critic KIA would have balanced things out a bit. Critics are forever being accused of killing plays, books, and restaurants. Isn't it only fair to turn the tables?

*Media Person wired the governors of sixteen Southern and Western states, proposing fugu as a more efficient replacement for electrocution: Not only does it cut down on power bills, but the condemned gets a gourmet last meal and execution of sentence at the same time.

When Worlds Collude

Media Person has discovered a new law explaining the workings of our universe, which, frankly, Media Person is just about fed up with.

The problem is there's more than one. Now Media Person knows a lot of you are saying, "Oh, no; here comes some silly science-fiction concept." Well, you're just going to have to face the nasty truth: There are at least two and maybe more parallel universes. And we seem to slide back and forth between them without any recognition of the shifting reality around us.

Media Person discovered this by reading the papers and watching TV news. How else can you explain all the times he has seen widely varying accounts of the same event? To believe they result from something as mundane as error is obviously preposterous. After all, we're talking about *journalists* here—sharp-witted, perceptive men and women trained to observe events and describe them in rich, precise detail. No, the reporters must have been in different worlds, or at least dimensions, where eerily similar but not identical news events were taking place.

Different worlds. This theory explains so many things. In one world, George Bush is Mr. Do-Nothing, a wimpy goofball who lacks vision and can't make a decision. In another, he's a tough, popular, principled president who acts judiciously, boldly, but always with compassion. In one world, America is the world's leading superpower, a country with a solid economy that has won the Cold War and is the envy of the earth. In another world, it's a fading, helpless giant, riddled by drugs, crime, debt, a rotting infrastructure, and immorality. In one world Hulk Hogan is a world champion athlete and the idol of millions; in another a strutting, vulgar clown in a phony freak show for suckers.

And then there is the case of the Wandering Mole. When the movie *She-Devil* opened, the nation's reviewers felt compelled to vividly describe a prosthetic facial growth sported by one of the leads, Roseanne Barr. Oddly they found it in different locations:

"A mole under her lower lip that looks like a surgically implanted raisin," said Roger Ebert.

"Her hairy upper lip (which also sports a mole the size of a Hershey's Kiss)" said David Edelstein, *New York Post*.

"She has a riveting black mole the size of a dime between her nose and upper lip," said Vincent Canby, *The New York Times*.

What was going on here? Apparently, different *She-Devil*s had been filmed for different universes with differing tastes. Of course, Media Person should have figured this whole thing out years ago. The evidence was staring him right in the face. How many reviews had he read where one critic said a movie was wonderful and another said it was terrible? Zillions. He could kick himself.

Now if only we knew how to identify these universes and choose which one to be in. Why, it's possible that lives could be saved. Say you get sick and need a hospital. In one universe, according to the *New York Daily News*,

A HOSPITAL STAY CAN HURT YOU, KILL YOU

In that universe under discussion, a report by New York State's Health Department revealed that "reportable incidents" in state hospitals—that is, accidents to patients or harmful treatment—

had risen over 50 percent since 1987. It was clear that something was desperately wrong.

But over in another, happier universe, New York hospitals were in much better shape. In this universe, which had been visited by the *Post*,

PATIENT INJURY RATE IN N.Y. HOSPITALS IS ON THE DECLINE

Here, the number of patients accidentally killed or maimed had *dropped* since 1987.

It was a sad day when Irving Berlin died but it became even sadder when Media Person read the papers and learned that actually, two Irving Berlins had died. They were very different men. In one universe, autodidactic Irv could only play the white keys on his piano. The parallel Berlin, according to the paper of that universe, could only play the black. One Berlin was the son of a rabbi, the other the son of a cantor. One Berlin had nurses at his side when he died, the other a doctor and a nurse.

On and on went the dueling Berlins. Though both had written "God Bless America," they had done it in different ways. Berlin number one went to see Kate Smith backstage at her popular radio show. He had trouble getting past the doorman but finally Smith's manager came out and Berlin told him, "I have a song for Kate Smith. I want to sing it for her." He did and she did and we did. Immortality.

Berlin number two was not as aggressive but, fortunately for him, the Kate Smith in his parallel universe was. His Kate, needing a patriotic song for Armistice Day, went looking for her Irving Berlin and found him. Berlin rummaged through his files and came up with "God Bless America" which, in this universe, he'd written twenty years before as a World War I doughboy and then forgotten.

Since reading these two versions from separate worlds, Media Person has always thought of the song as "Gods Bless Americas."

Large segments of the population act very different from their parallel-universe counterparts. American schoolchildren, for example. In one universe, they are hopeless idiots. Every week another shocking survey comes out documenting yet another vital area in which they are utterly ignorant. They can't read. They can't add. They think New Zealand is just south of Vermont and Canada Dry is the capital of Egypt. They believe Dan Quayle plays shortstop for the Phillies and quarks are a rock group. But every week in the parallel universe, an American teenager cracks the code of some sophisticated computer in the Pentagon or a major money-center bank. Media Person is not sure which group is more frightening.

New York newspapers in particular seem prone to having their reporters fall into alternate universes where events start the same but suddenly veer off onto rapidly diverging rails.

One day, for instance, the NBC network held a press conference. This much everyone agreed on. The next day, the *Post* headlined:

NBC EXECUTIVES DEFEND THEIR PROGRAMMING WAYS

TARTIKOFF, WRIGHT SAY THEY WON'T AVOID CONTROVERSIAL

ISSUES

The *Daily News* headlined:

NBC TO PLAY IT SAFER

Obviously different worlds. Another time, a *New York Newsday* story on foreign relations began:

President George Bush yesterday welcomed Soviet leader Mikhail Gorbachev's unexpected letter proposing a "constructive dialogue" with Western democracies at the economic summit, saying it was "just one more manifestation of the exciting times we're in of change" in East-West relations.

Post lead, same day:

A boyishly exuberant President Bush yesterday brushed off Soviet chief Mikhail Gorbachev's surprise letter asking for closer economic ties to the top capitalist nations as "a little premature."

It was the Double Bush thing again. Bush the Tough was presiding in one universe and the kinder, gentler Bush in the other. The two separate countries both coincidentally named "China" also evince split personalities, if these two same-day headlines, the first from *The New York Times*, the second from *New York Newsday*, are any indication:

BEIJING INSISTS KHMER ROUGE SHARE IN RULE

CHINA VOWS TO STOP AIDING CAMBODIA'S KHMER ROUGE

That the parallel universes may be basically divided into a tough, hardline world and a nice, soft world is one possibility that scientists should be looking into. This idea hit Media Person with particular force the day the killer bees lost their sting.

As you may know, the Freddy Krueger of the insect world was invented in the secret tabloid laboratories of Australian media monster Rupert Murdoch for the purpose of increasing newspaper circulation. Killer bees were then loosed—in a brilliant stratagem—upon South America. Ravaging the hapless locals and spreading terror as well as banner headlines, the bees worked their way inexorably north toward a cowering USA. Tabloid readers knew it was only a matter of time till the vast, buzzing cloud of horror enveloped us, bringing millions of innocent Americans a hideous, writhing death by multiple, tiny, toxic punctures.

After an inexplicable period of quiescence (during which, coincidentally, Murdoch had grown more interested in the movie and TV entertainment business than newspapers) killer bees were rediscovered by *USA Today*. While its front-page story did supply the mandatory map showing the swarm approaching the U.S. border, somehow the old terror was missing. The little nippers just didn't seem as scary as they used to in the tabloids.

Instead of inspiring fear, as proper killer-bee headlines should, *USA Today*'s quoted experts who advised

BE "INFORMED," NOT "TERRIFIED"

DISRUPTION TO CROPS "IS MORE OF A CONCERN
THAN THE 'KILLER' THING"

Disruption to crops? This is the menace we've dreaded for decades? They're going to harass *plants*? What a letdown. Media

Person was crushed till he realized that *USA Today*'s killer bees must be from the gentle universe and that those of the fierce universe were just as nasty as ever and would probably be back as soon as some tabloid reporter stumbled across the dimensional divide into the world where killer bees still kill for a thrill.

Yes, different worlds are here to stay, and the implications are not pleasant. Any time you leave home, you don't know if you're walking into, say, New York Timesworld or Wall Street Journa-Land, where things look kind of genteel, solemn, and formal, where Anthony Lewis or George Will might buttonhole you and wish to discuss missile-reduction talks, or if you're heading for Tabloidsville, where you might be macheted by a gang of thirteen-year-old girls and lie bleeding and despoiled on the sidewalk for fifty-five minutes before a broken-down ambulance arrives and rattles through potholed streets to an overcrowded hospital where you expire because your gurney was left in an elevator by mistake.

This is yet one more reason why Media Person never leaves his apartment, where he feels safe and calm and . . . Hey, wait a minute. What if there are several different Media Persons in several alternate universes? And what if they've all written books? And what if the *Read My Clips* you're reading is an inferior version?

The only way you could tell is if this chapter becomes ashamed of itself and quits in the middle of th

Ayatollah You So

When Salman Rushdie was sentenced to death by Iran on a first-degree writing rap, which caused a worldwide uproar, one result was a boom in the commentary market. Few went so far as to actually read *The Satanic Verses* but everyone had something to say about it. And so Media Person had to say something, too. Actually, three things:

1. A number of contemplative commentators commented that we in the West don't grasp how sacred the Koran is to Muslims and that any perceived ridicule is intolerable to them. True, but on the other hand, the Muslims don't grasp how much we in the West cherish the right to ridicule things that others hold sacred.

In Show-Biz America, the nation that loves to kid around, most things in public life eventually end up as a joke in a late-night TV monologue. Indeed, many Americans have no other way of communicating but jokes, which is why such a large segment of the populace is employed as comedians. We're just big kids. Tell us we can't mock something and we just want to tweak it harder. Why should we respect Islam? We don't respect anything. To us, God is a comedy character played by George Burns. The president is a Johnny Carson joke. Our cultural life is one big, ongoing celebrity roast, and ridicule is our holy writ, satire our sacrament. If Ayatollah Khomeini had ever heard what late-night American TV routinely said about him, he would have sentenced the entire Western Hemisphere to death.

2. In case the Shiites were contemplating condemning more writers, Media Person called for immediate creation of a federal writers' protection program. Fugitive authors would be given new faces, homes, and even new literary identities to evade detection. Under such a program, Rushdie, for instance, might resurface in Walla Walla as Saul D. Rushman, writing novels about his Hasidic boyhood in Flatbush.

3. When the late Ayatollah Khomeini announced that whoever assassinated Rushdie would go to heaven, Media Person immediately wired the inimitable imam expressing his surprise to learn that the admissions committee awards points for bagging novelists. MP specifically wanted to know if it was just Rushdie or if he could crash paradise with a potshot at Judith Krantz or Sidney Sheldon. Unfortunately he never received a reply.

Drop That Magazine and Take Off Your Clothes

The phone rang and someone was screaming in agony. It was Leg Person, whom Media Person occasionally employs to glance at things in the outside world and report back.

"What's the matter?" said Media Person.

"I can't straighten up," said Leg Person. "I was just handed the heaviest press kit in journalism history and it doubled me over. Damn thing must weigh forty pounds."

She'd gone to attend a press conference/lunch held by Whittle Communications, the most dangerous company in the world, working incessantly to spread advertising to new venues.

As the affair was being held at the Four Seasons restaurant, Media Person immediately cut to the heart of the issue.

"How's the food?" he said.

"Pretty good for a freebie," said Leg Person. "Prosciutto and pears. Chicken breast. Cake with chocolate chips. Fattening sauces. Whittle's really going deep-pocket on this outing. They ran a promo film done for them by the Maysles Brothers."

Media Person grunted as if moderately impressed.

"Well, actually, the Maysles Brother. There's only one left. Anyway, here was this stark, trendy, handheld camera, cinema-verité documentary, and what's it about? *Magazine editors*. It's as if Stravinsky wrote a jingle for Bud Lite."

"Now this whole deal is about some new magazine that goes to doctors' waiting rooms?" said Media Person.

"Six new magazines," Leg Person said. "And six different subjects: health, personalities, sports, fiction, family, and living. The advertisers seem to love it. Chris Whittle said he sold eighty million dollars in advertising before the first issue even comes out. But the competition hates it. There's this exclusivity clause."

"The doctor isn't allowed to have any other magazines in his office, is that it?"

"Two," said Leg Person. "He can keep two others."

"Yeah? What if he sneaks in a third? Does Whittle send some goons over to slap the quack around? 'Hand over that *National Geographic*, you cheating son of a bitch!' "

"I don't know," said Leg Person. "I didn't ask about punishment. But here's something interesting. The magazines are designed to be read in thirty minutes."

"What happens if the nurse says, 'The doctor will see you now,' and you've only been reading twenty minutes and you're in the middle of an article?"

"Couldn't happen at my doctor," said Leg Person. "I could read all six. But you could always stuff the thing in your purse when the nurse is taking someone's urine sample. Or you could finish on the way out—if you're not too drugged or in pain from seeing the bill."

"Is this the future?" Media Person pondered in his pseudo-philosophical way. "This marketing gimmick, what do they call it?"

"Targeted marketing."

"Is that where magazines are headed?"

"If you believe Chris Whittle."

"So," said Media Person. "The future is you want to read a magazine, you go to the doctor? Or the tax accountant? Like if you're a Morton Kondracke fan you have to fake a virus every week to see him in *The New Republic*? A reading habit could bankrupt you faster than cocaine."

"You really think there are Morton Kondracke fans?" said Leg Person.

Media Person ignored the question. "If this is the future, I'd better glimpse it," he said. "Let's see the samples."

"Forget it," said Leg Person. "No way am I schlepping this monstrosity any farther. You want to read this press kit, you'll find the box in the phone booth at the Four Seasons. If I were you, I'd bring help."

John Wayne Is Dead but Lovelier Than Ever

Media Person has just been alerted to a crime that could occur only in this nation in this century.*

He became aware of the problem, as he has become aware of so many problems, while watching *Donahue*. It is, in fact, *Donahue*'s chief virtue to assure people suffering from dumb problems that there is always someone with a problem even dumber.

Telling Phil their grievances was a panel of angry descendants of dead celebrities. It seems that the likenesses of their famous ancestors had been pirated by unscrupulous profiteers.

John Wayne, Jr., was complaining that some lowdown, yellow-bellied, capitalist varmint was selling postcards of John Wayne, Sr.—doctored to make him appear to be wearing *lipstick*.

Media Person considered becoming incensed, as the younger Wayne was inviting him to do. Sure, advertisers constantly steal our favorite music, rip off great scenes from movies, and turn

---

*That's the United States in the twentieth, for anyone digging up this book in archaeological excavations.

Washington and Lincoln into department-store shills—but this was different. This was The Duke, everyone's boyhood hero. And they were trifling with his *masculinity*. It did seem a bit un-American.

But hold on . . . something crossed Media Person's mind. He feverishly burrowed into Mount Media and finally found what he was looking for, a recent issue of *Premiere*, the glossy movie mag from the Rupert Murdoch empire. In it was an ad from the Franklin Mint offering "the John Wayne Armed Forces Commemorative," a framed replica of the .45-caliber pistol "he carried in so many great military films."

When Media Person had first seen the ad, he'd paid it little heed, simply wondering what type of primitive mentality would shell out $395 for this pseudocollectible. What pride of ownership could anyone derive from possessing a *copy* of a *prop* used by a performer *pretending* to be a war hero?

Was this atrocity yet another ripoff of John Wayne's image? Nope. The Armed Forces Commemorative was officially authorized by the Wayne family. Said so right on the page. This was legit.

Oh, now Media Person got it. It's wrong for outsiders to peddle rubbish exploiting the good name and reputation of a beloved star. But it's perfectly okay for the family to do the same thing.

Hear the Trumps
Blare

In the summer of 1988 it became clear that Donald Trump, the world's noisiest billionaire, had made another major acquisition—now he owned the media.

You couldn't open a newspaper or turn on a TV set without hearing about Trump's magnificent new yacht, Trump's splendiferous hotels, Trump's fabulously blond wife, Trump's best-selling autobiography, and Trump's sponsorship of a heavyweight championship bout at Trump's gambling casino in Trump's Atlantic City in the state of New Trumpsey.

Still to be announced was the deal that would establish Trump the Planet, making all the rest of us Trumplings, with rent due each month to His Trumpness.

The media were full of sycophantic praise. In her "Step Into My Parlor" column in *Cosmopolitan*, the perennially breathless Helen Gurley Brown issued a full report on her visit to the Trump estate in Palm Beach, Florida. So hard did she *kvell*, Media Person feared the magazine would overflow, scalding him with hot, italicized gush.

Brown had stepped into Trump's parlor, looked up, and nearly died of excitement. Describing the gleaming gold-leaf ceiling, she giddily reported: "They don't *do* that anymore; twenty-six people climb up there between June and October when the house is empty and clean it with toothbrushes and *mineral* water."

Wasn't it exactly this type of thing that once caused the French peasantry to go into the guillotine business?

Brown accorded the Trumps the reverence usually reserved in holy books for creators of universes. "Some (jealous) people are waiting (and waiting and WAITING) for a serious flaw to emerge," HGB writes of her host and hostess. "It just isn't *emerging*."

Perhaps it's possible, if Media Person may offer a *(teensy)* suggestion, that B*r*o*w*n wasn't, you know, *LOOKING HARD ENOUGH*!!!?

The only things Media Person saw emerging from the Trump empire were monumental greed, colossal arrogance, bad taste, and a compulsive need to show off, but, okay, look, maybe those aren't serious flaws in modern society. God knows, Media Person doesn't get out much.

Next, the unfortunately irrepressible Ted Turner announced that he would make Trump the Film. Every organ of mass information immediately rushed to blab the news of this dubious enterprise to the public. Was this necessary? Who besides the Mad Colorizer would want to sit through a Donald Trump vanity biopic? It sounded like a deal engineered by Sid, the Hollywood hack from Garry Trudeau's *Doonesbury*. *Great concept. Toss in Eddie Murphy, a coupla broads, and a car chase, and we've got us a smash.*

As the summer wore on, the self-aggrandizing landlord spent more and more time flying swarms of media suck-ups to his Trumped-up castles and circuses. His new thirty-million-dollar yacht, the size of Saturn, was on the cover of *New York* magazine and was praised by Liz Smith, the syndicated gossip columnist, for its "tasteful beauty." This was the vessel with the tortoiseshell ceiling in the master stateroom, the disco, and 235 telephones.

Finally, the onslaught of Trumpery drove Media Person temporarily mad. He began fulminating and ranting. It was a very unpleasant thing to see and you should be glad you weren't around.

"Can one day go by in this city without a planted story, an oozing column, a TV feature, a hundred gossip items and photos about Trump and his relatives and his possessions?" raved Media Person in the doomed column he wrote for several exquisite years in the tragically ill-fated 7 Days magazine in order to pay for cable TV and his favorite beverage—apple-cinnamon-flavored tea with honey.

This little diatribe brought an avalanche of mail.

Well, actually, there was one letter, but it was sincere. It was from Liz Smith, still a syndicated gossip columnist just as she was four paragraphs ago, who conceded that "overkill is a cardinal sin," but asked, "What is the media to do with the Ts when they keep 'making news'?"

The public goes wild for the Trumps, she claimed—"they are like movie stars"—so how can the press not cover them?

This was a legitimate, thoughtful question, the kind of question Media Person hates. When Media Person has got himself really worked up denouncing some rabid publicity hog, there is nothing more annoying than being slowed down by attempts at logic.

No, Media Person was not about to back down on this issue. He came up with what he thought was a sensible solution: How about if the media simply never mention Trump again?

If the public does in fact think of the Trumps as movie stars, Media Person reasoned, isn't it because their immense publicity machine has craftily crafted their image that way and the media has bought in and amplified it?

Hadn't the media really created this monster and wasn't it thus the media's responsibility to destroy him? Wouldn't it be the height of irresponsibility to let him walk the earth, buying it piece by piece? Certainly if the man saw one week go by with no mention of himself in press or television, he'd fold up like a doughnut with the jelly sucked out.

It seemed to Media Person the perfect solution to an increasingly ugly problem. He was confident that the media would see the beauty of the plan and take him up on it.

The idea was completely ignored and Trump got more press than ever.

The hoohah that broke out early in 1990 when Trump announced he was deacquisitioning his semibeautiful, fortyish wife, Ivana, and was revealed to be dallying with a younger, blonder model/actress/mistress named Marla Maples, made the earlier stuff seem as nothing. The front pages were filled with Trumpage for weeks.

While the tabloids joyously rolled around in the sexy muck, the more respectable organs such as *Time* and *The New York Times* sniffed at the spectacle in disdain while managing to print the juicy details in the guise of media analysis.

As a result of all this, Donald Trump became even more powerful, vulgar, and spiritually bloated than ever* and the rest of humanity was correspondingly impoverished as the world turned into a trashy wasteland devoid of humane values or any legitimate reason to continue existing.

It wasn't Media Person's fault, he can tell you that.

---

*Two years later the bottom dropped out of the real-estate market, and Trump suddenly lost his all-important Air of Invincibility. Not twenty-four hours later, Donald Trump had been deflated and dismantled, his vital organs shipped to a warehouse in Hackensack, N.J. Most of the media cackled in glee, pretended they had hated Trump all along, and blamed his preposterous rise on the bankers.

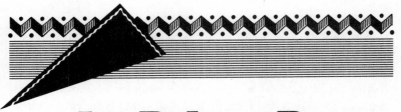

Let Bylines Be Bygones

Something was wrong with *The New York Times*. Media Person had been thinking this for maybe ten or fifteen years but couldn't put his finger on what it was. Suddenly, it hit him.

Bylines.

The great bylines were gone. For years, they had been Media Person's favorite part of the *Times*, the grand, imposing, patrician names that gave it character and weight. Names like McCandlish Phillips, Bosley Crowther, Edith Evans Asbury, Brooks Atkinson, Turner Catledge. Or was it Catledge Turner? No matter, the typical *Times* byline could be reversed with no resultant loss of grandeur.

These imposing sobriquets signaled that the news had dignity and importance despite its ephemeral nature. In fact, you didn't even need the news; you could just read the names and feel nourished. Why, *Brooks Atkinson* had such weight it later became the name of a building.

Many *Times* bylines evoked a bucolic romp through the hunt country: Sylvan Fox, Farnsworth Fowles, Carter B. Horsley. Of this great genre, only Fox Butterfield remains.

In the old days, the *Times* would have snapped up the young J. Danforth Quayle, scion of an Indiana newspaper family, in a flash. (He probably would have avoided being a war correspondent.)

And there were other, more exotic monikers—Vartanig Vartan and Pranay Gupte come to mind—that you could chant soothingly like mantras. These, and the various Abes (most, like A. M. Rosenthal, trying to suppress their ethnicity with initials) seemed to represent the upward-striving sons and daughters of immigrants fighting for a place among the snooty aristos. Wasn't that what America was all about?

Where are the signatures of yesteryear? They've mostly expired, like Anatole Broyard, or retired or hired to other employment. Ada Louise Huxtable has scribbled off to the editorial board or someplace. A few remain. John Noble Wilford, Wolfgang Saxon, and Isadore Barmash still resonate, and of course there is the imperiously Teutonic Christopher Lehmann-Haupt.

But the other bylines have gone bye-bye.

You find lots of new names in the *Times* these days, but they are bland, anonymous, yuppielike tags of no substance. They fail to trip the eye.* You slide by them unseeing, subliminally starved. You are filled with a nameless sorrow.

*With the exception of Esther B. Fein, which answers the question, "How Esther be?"

Meek Hail Gorby Show

Media Person was remote dancing and suddenly here was Joan Rivers watering her talk show. An unappetizing spectacle, let him tell you.

Tears of Rivers poured forth. It seems some dastardly pseudonymous writer in *GQ* had accused Rivers of behaving callously in regard to the suicide of her husband. Now here she was crying onscreen and suing off.

You know, if Media Person had grown rich, famous, and less ugly by making cruel remarks about other people (and don't think he hasn't tried) he wouldn't have the chutzpah to sue somebody for fifty million, as Joan Rivers did, for attributing some more cruel remarks to her.

Not only did these calumnious libels hurt her and her daughter, Joan sobbed, they could actually damage her as-yet unborn great-grandchildren.

Now here was an interesting new legal doctrine: Posterity damage. Under this, a jury could set aside several million dollars to compensate any Rivers descendant who might happen to rocket-skate into the Beverly Hills Library and Hot Tub Center in April of 2320, stumble on compact teledisks screaming out Great-great-granny's shame, and be humiliated in front of anyone tuning in on the telepathy channel.

A private detective apparently hired by Joan or her lawyers tried to unmask the *GQ* cad by asking journalist friends to phone around and see if they could dig up anything.

Wouldn't it have been easier just to monitor the other talk shows? Whoever wrote the piece would eventually turn up on one to chat about it. Everyone does.

Sooner or later even Mikhail Gorbachev will—provided he avoids assassination or impeachment long enough. So far he's restricted his American TV appearances to interviews with people like Tom Brokaw, who was such a softie that some newspaper columnists foamed at the mouth. William Safire said the interview was "an hourlong exhibition of obsequious arrogance, cunning manipulation, evasive bullying and outright dishonesty."

For a moment, Media Person thought it must have been an interview with George Steinbrenner.

But what really burned Safire's toast was a Gallup poll revealing that twice as many Americans have a "favorable opinion of Gorbachev as have an unfavorable opinion of him."

Come on, Bill. Give your fellow citizens a little credit. This doesn't mean Americans are ready to elect Gorbachev president. It just means that we saw him on TV and we like his act. And why shouldn't we? He has more charisma than George Bush and so far he's underexposed.

Remember, what counts in Show-Biz America is entertainment value, not substance. By ratifying Gorbachev in the Gallup poll, we're giving him approval to appear on our talk shows.

Let's see how he handles himself with Phil, Oprah, Johnny, Dave, Geraldo, Sally, and Jessy. Let's see how he reacts when Joan demands that he describe his first sexual experience. Or when Oprah hugs him. Then, by God, we'll know instinctively if perestroika's for real or just another sneaky commie plot to catch us unawares, slip through our defenses, and nuke us into oblivion.

Let's see if Gorbachev can sing, dance, or do a passable imitation of Kurt Waldheim forgetting he was a Nazi. Then we'll know if Gorby's a good guy or bad guy.

When it comes to assessing political character, America has the true test, if only we realize it and dare to use it. Someday we must.

Hunting the Elusive Quayle

Media Person was trying to compose a letter to Eugene T. Maleska when a concerned reader called to complain that *Time* had gone gaga.

"What does it mean?" cried the concerned reader. "They've put in an interview section and expanded the people section and the index. And the pictures are getting bigger and bigger. What have they done to *Time*?"

"Don't panic," said Media Person. "This is simply further evidence of Media Person's Theory of Magazine Evolution, which states that all magazines are gradually turning into the same magazine, namely, *People*."

"Oh my God," said the concerned reader.

"It's true," said Media Person. "The future is fluff. A corollary theory posits that all newspapers are gradually turning into *USA Today*, which itself is turning into a television show, though not so gradually."

The concerned reader made indescribably sickening noises and hung up.

Curious, Media Person burrowed around the base of Mount Media, the majestic pile of magazines and newspapers rising near him to a snow-covered peak, until he found the new, improved *Time*.

Fittingly the cover story was about television, specifically the decline of the networks. This gave the art director a chance to employ many splotches of color, send whiz-bang laser rays flying around the three network logos and also prominently display the fun word *ZAPPED*. It was keen. You could dance to it.

Inside, a letter from the managing editor assured Media Person that, despite all the merriment, *Time*'s mission was still to increase our knowledge of the world.

"It is still 1988," the managing editor confidently asserted, no doubt after thorough research, "but I think we are in fact well on our way to a magazine for the 1990s, a vital print companion to an electronic age."

It sounded to Media Person like the guy really wanted to be a TV producer.

Media Person tried to return to his letter to Eugene T. Maleska, who had greatly annoyed him, but the phone rang again. It was another reader, and this one sounded scared.

"Beware," said the scared reader. "There is great danger. I just read in the papers that Quayle has escaped his handlers. He is on the loose."

"I know," said Media Person, who had been following the election campaign with much interest, as well as nausea. "I read it, too. Something snapped inside him and, ping! he was gone, campaigning as he pleased, *actually talking to reporters on his own.*"

"It's terrifying," said the scared reader. "I'm afraid to watch TV news. You see, I'm a Republican. He could turn up anywhere and say anything. *Anything*. You know [and here the man's voice faded to a dark whisper], Quayle doesn't live in this century."

Media Person was aware of this. Quayle had admitted it at a news conference. Asked his opinion of the Holocaust, he'd explained that it was "an obscene period in our nation's history." Everyone looked at him oddly, so he said what he meant was "this *century's* history." Then, to irrevocably clarify matters, he added: "We all lived in this century. I didn't live in this century."

The scared reader said he was so worried he'd called Republican Spin Control, the agency in charge of explaining to the press what candidates *really* meant after they said something that might be misunderstood or, worse, not misunderstood. "They told me they expect to have Quayle back in custody soon because the Secret Service and the press corps were both scouring the country for him."

"Quayle's not even the worst of it," Media Person said. "I read in a science article somewhere—maybe *Penthouse*—that the candidates are such small men running such a trivial campaign that our country is being diminished by it. We've already lost an estimated one hundred twenty-six thousand square miles, and more land goes every day."

The scared reader said he had to check his property and hung up. Before Media Person could get back to his Maleska letter, the front-door intercom shrieked. It was Mail Person. She had a package for Media Person. It was from *Corporate Finance*, which sounds like a government tax bureau but is really a magazine and which was blatantly attempting to bribe Media Person with a huge slab of chocolate about the size of *National Geographic* stamped with the magazine's title logo. Of course, keeping gifts is strictly against Media Person's ethical standards.

So he biochemically processed the illicit freebie and recycled it into the ecosystem. The phone rang again. It was an irate reader. Media Person has an excellent relationship with his readers. They often feel free to call him with their questions, comments, and advice. Media Person feels free to insult them.

"Hey," said the guy irately. "How come in Saturday's *Post*, page eight was identical to page four?"

"New cost-cutting policy," Media Person said. "It's sort of like TV reruns. If you liked page four the first time, you'll probably enjoy reading it again."

"Smartass," said the irate guy and hung up. Would these interruptions never cease? Apparently not. Here was yet another ring.

"This is Eugene T. Maleska," a voice said. "The crossword-puzzle editor of *The New York Times*."

Media Person was temporarily at a loss.

"I was just reading about how you keep trying to write me a letter," said Maleska, "and I'm wondering if I'm ever going to find out what you want."

"Sure," said Media Person, striking a tone that he thought was irritable but fair. "I've got some cross words for you. That puzzle last Sunday? Listen, I didn't mind *rigel*. I didn't mind *telpher*. I didn't even mind *chevet*, *apices*, *barm*, *spile*, *guipure*, or *colberteen*. But I must tell you, sir: with *foolish guillemot*, you went too fucking far."

Eugene T. Maleska hung up. Editors are so thin-skinned.

Star Warts

Stuart doesn't drink or do drugs. He's normal. He has a job. When he comes home from work, I might make a salmon or a sea bass in papillote, laced with lots of garlic and dill, and a big salad. Then I like to read or watch a movie or have wild and imaginative sex. —MARGAUX HEMINGWAY, in *People*

Yeah, Media Person knows what she means. His life is much like Margaux's, except for the wild and imaginative sex (though he has often imagined wild sex) and the sea bass in papillote (What *is* papillote, exactly?) and the fact that he's never made the Betty Ford Center.

But Media Person often thinks about the Betty Ford Center. And the thing he wonders is: Does anyone ever go there and just shut up about it? Or is it mandatory to check out, pick up your luggage, walk across the lobby to *People* magazine's truth booth, and spill your guts?

What we're really talking about here is the celebrity profile, without which there could be no journalism in the twentieth century.

Up until around the late '6os, celebrity profiles were mostly puff pieces, exercises in adulation, extensions of the celebrity's effort to plug the new movie, record, or TV show. Then things changed. Writers like Gay Talese in *Esquire* and several others who are going to be really miffed that Media Person left them out, pioneered a new technique: honesty. It was bracing. It was fun to read. It spread. It spread so much that celebrity profiles became a journalistic staple, then a glut, and finally a bore. Today they are back to being puff pieces that plug movies again—but with an interesting difference.

Performers have become more candid about revealing their flaws. In fact, now they revel in them. They're not blind to the fact that problems and frailties are good copy and make them seem colorful and interesting. The odd thing, though, is that the horrors they recount to the press are always in the past. Nothing bad is ever happening in a celebrity's life *right now*.

The plot of the generic celebrity profile can be outlined as follows:

I. You can't believe what a mess Barry Boldface was. His hideous nightmare of a life had become one long depraved orgy of (pick one or two): A. Booze, B. Gambling, C. Dope, D. Unsafe sex, E. Wanton, savage weight gain.

II. Then Barry found (pick one): A. God, B. Betty Ford, C. His new wife or lover, D. His new personal trainer, E. Shrink, F. Guru, G. The all-fungus diet, H. His newborn baby, who kind of put everything in perspective and made him realize what's really important.

This saved his life.

III. Now Barry's normal, calm, in his best shape ever, totally centered, sensitive to the needs of his fellow human beings, and experiencing great happiness, love, and personal growth.

IV. Oh and by the way, he's just finished a new film that everyone thinks is by far his best work yet. Roll the clip.

The I-Used-to-Be-a-Mess pseudoconfessional has become the dominant theme of modern celebrity interviewing. Of course there are other themes such as Not Just Another Pretty Face. This story appears when a starlet graduates to full stardom. It asserts that she (or occasionally, he) is not only good-looking but—miracle of miracles—can actually act. Talk about multifaceted personalities! As acting is her job, it's a little hard to understand why this claim should cause amazement, but apparently it does. When Michelle Pfeiffer did her publicity tour for her breakthrough picture *Married to the Mob*, the Pretty Face motif was a must for profilers. *Premiere*'s story was headlined "Beyond the Beautiful Face" and the *New York Post*'s was "She's More than Just Another Gorgeous Face."

Stars who manage to stay around long enough to make another movie after the Not-Just-a-Pretty-Face phase may well be promoted to the Fighting-the-Stereotype class. That popular profile motif goes something like this:

> Sick of playing hookers who go to medical school and become top neurosurgeons in her last four films, Laura Lissome quit working for sixteen months until a nonstereotypical role came along.
>
> "It was worth the wait," she says.
>
> In her new movie, *Habeas Corpse*, Lissome plays a lady cabbie who goes to law school and becomes a tough big-city D.A. who falls in love with a Mafia don.

Seldom encountered anymore is the good old, flat-out, gore-spewing hatchet job. This entertaining if brutal genre joyfully discloses that some bright, lovable, talented star is in truth a boorish dolt who got ahead by mutilating his children on orders from Satan. It has faded as celebrity journalism has more and more become an adjunct of the great show-biz publicity machine, whose overseers do not believe that trashing stars sells tickets.

Celebrities on the cover also sell magazines, and today's canny star demands more control before offering up his or her fabulous mug. Most stars give interviews only when pushing their latest movie. The hotter ones increasingly want cover-or-nothing, and some demand—and get—approval over photos, quotes, and writer selection, formerly sacrosanct journalistic prerogatives. A reporter who writes a negative piece won't be writing many more.

Those who do write celebrity profiles tend to be highly impressed with themselves, but only at the outset. To lunch with some bronzed icon while everyone else in the restaurant, pretending to keep their faces in their goat-cheese salads, is really sneaking peeks in your direction, is heady stuff. But after a few more I-Used-to-Be-a-Monster-But-Hey-Get-a-Loada-Me-Now pieces, the reporter realizes that the star now being so charming and friendly will have forgotten his name and face an hour later, as will the maître d', should the reporter ever have the effrontery to enter the bistro again on his own. Eventually the celebrity reporter becomes a depressed, cynical, self-hating wretch who eventually may need to check into the Betty Ford Center himself.

Unfortunately, since he's not a celebrity, he can't get in.

To Sleep, Perchance to Scream

Oh God.

What time is it?

Media Person stirs. He wakes. Something is terribly wrong.

Some noxious yellow vapor pours into his bedroom. It's . . . *daylight*.

The horror.

Why is Media Person up at this unCarsonly hour? His slumber should last past noon. Late to bed, late to rise makes a man miss morning, when being up hurts his eyes.

Rousted untimely by forces unknown, Media Person staggers toward coffee, reflexively flipping on the TV without even noticing.

Vapid presences beam at him. He fumbles for the remote, tries zapping them away, but ghostly yappers haunt all channels, different yet the same.

Who are these offensively chipper humanoids?

Media Person shakes off the sleep, thinks hard. He recalls the old tribal myths: Weird tales of the one called Garroway, companion to an ape. Lurid japes of a fat man in a toupee and an insane grin. And he known as Hartman, too dull to live yet somehow alive. Media Person has never really believed that television could exist before noon, yet here it is, small as life.

Shallow prattle emanating from smiling mannequins, happy-faced but, underneath, oddly tense.

Why do they chill him so? What is this half-buried remembrance of helpless, creeping terror?

Of course. As the truth hits him, Media Person involuntarily shudders. *School*. The truth is morning television feels like school. Fear clutches Media Person's guts. His screams rend the thin morning air.

The last time he saw people behaving this way was that endless era when he was forced to attend morning. Neat, scrubbed, ever so alert and perky, their earnest faces straining to show that they are *really interested* in the dull proceedings at hand, these guys are in class.

Media Person is fully awake now, bathed in the satisfying horror of an ugly perception. Yes, he well remembers the stifling, chalky taste of forced attention and politeness masking boredom, tension, competition, and fear.

The same rigid scheduling prevails: If a subject somehow gets interesting, too bad, bell rings, change class.

The same people prevail: On top are teacher's pets, glib, eager to please, always ready to speak up brightly and mouth the conventional wisdom, not offend, not challenge authority.

And there are cutups, but here only cute, harmless ones. No delinquents or sexpots or sulkers or sloppy dressers allowed. No reality.

The weatherguy puts on a silly hat. He says something pleasant (but not witty) to the blandly blondly beautiful anchors, who chirp back in kind. They all beam at one another, but it's our approval they want, the unseen teacher.

Why is this torture allowed to exist? Why do people take this dreary banality?

Because, Media Person finally realizes, of the universal nightmare. The one everyone has: being back in school, taking tests not studied for, being called on and going blank, being imprisoned forever. The morning audience has just come from the old nightmare into wakefulness. Now it can tune in for a while and then, thank God, *turn it off*.

The relief must be incredible.

Whew. This was exhausting. Media Person's eyelids grow heavy now from the exertion. Delicious tendrils of sleep fondle his brain lobes, just as they always did in the classroom. Rescue is near. Others must go work but Media Person can shirk. The noble head nods. The empty babble is fading to a whisper.

Media Person drops off, drops out.

Letter Boxing

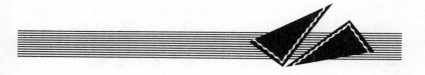

Dear Ann Landers:

You know that poignant confession you ran from the lifelong compulsive liar who said his lies had led to broken marriages, crime, and prison? And how you replied that this was a great lesson for people who play fast and loose with the truth?

But, Ann—how can we believe a guy who admits he's a liar? What if his lying ways really brought him wealth, privilege, and sexual satisfaction? What if he's sitting there right now laughing his two faces off at you and me?

In the future, Ann, please try to think things through more carefully before jumping to simpleminded moralistic conclusions that are at best naïve and at worst capable of driving some readers (like this one) into violent screaming rages that raise the stress level and possibly shorten one's lifespan.

Media Person

Dear Fox Network:

Has Media Person got a TV series for you.

This can't-miss concept was inspired by the fabulously sleazy unauthorized Jackie O bio that Media Person read excerpts of in all the tabloids. Already you're plotzing, right?

The idea hit MP right in the face: JFK's love life is classic, zany slapstick farce! What we have on our hands here is a surefire, solid-gold sitcom: *Jack and Jackie!*

Here's a summary of the pilot script, which is enclosed:

It starts with Jack (I see John Ritter—this kind of pratfall shtick is his forte) getting an alarm from the Secret Service: Jackie (Connie Chung is interested) is back from shopping! Her limo is pulling into the White House driveway. Omigod! Panic at poolside. Aides shove the giggling nude starlets out the back door, the champagne bottles and marijuana butts are swept up, the Sinatra music is cut and Jack and his houseguest, Charles de Gaulle (Jamie Farr), pull on their clothes just as Jackie walks in and the boys make like they're talking foreign policy, but she finds a bra under the diving board and blows her stack! From there it only gets funnier.

Trust me, this thing will be bigger than Lucy.

Media Person

Dear Miss Manners:

Media Person adores you. Oops, was that a breach of etiquette? We haven't been formally introduced, so perhaps Media Person shouldn't take such liberties. But he can't help himself. Every time he reads your refined, elegant column, he trembles and loses control of himself. He loves your gentle but firm manner, the witty way you scold the impolite, your unflinching willingness to make boors toe the line.

How Media Person looks forward to your weekly disciplinings. What heaven it would be if you could personally reform Media Person's errant behavior. Just a raised eyebrow, signaling your displeasure, would go a long way to correcting his many shortcomings, but an occasional light spanking or touch of the whip would further abjure the very naughty Media Person to mind his manners.

Breathlessly awaiting your reply and praying he hasn't offended your exquisite sensibilities, he remains your humble, obedient, groveling servant,

Media Person

Dear Marilyn vos Savant:

You are the smartest person in the universe. Media Person knows this because every Sunday he faithfully reads your "Ask Marilyn" column, which reaches nearly seventy million people every week in *Parade*, the Sunday supplement famous for its intellectually challenging articles as well as its ads for hand-crafted, museum-quality, porcelain reproductions of Dumbo the Flying Elephant. *Parade* always points out that you are listed in the *Guinness Book of World Records* under "Highest IQ."

So Media Person was disappointed by the answer you gave the reader who inquired if it's a good thing to know when you're going to die. You said it is. "Just think of the sheer joy of knowing," you wrote. "Why, you could take up *parachuting* if you wanted to."

Marilyn, if Media Person didn't know that you had the highest IQ anywhere, he would have found this answer spectacularly dumb.

Because you overlooked something. Okay, you take up parachuting because you know your date with death is far in the future, so a fatal accident is out of the question. You hit the sky, your chute fails to open, you arrive in a parking lot at 347 miles per hour and end up on a respirator paralyzed from the nose down with tubes sticking out of every orifice of your body, the unpleasant state in which you'll be spending the next forty-six years. But the good news is you're not dead.

You just wish you were.

Media Person

Dear Andre the Giant:

The curse of Media Person's life is that he's forever getting clever ideas that are useless to him but never gets a clever idea when he needs one. For instance, Media Person was just sitting here twiddling his thumbs (and by the way, is it possible to twiddle anything else or is twiddling a thumbs-only activity?) when it hit him that a great name for a woman wrestler would be Auntie Maim.

Unfortunately, Media Person doesn't know any wrestlers, male or female, and has no ties to the industry. He hopes you can pass on the idea to some deserving young muscular woman just starting her career. Media Person hates to see a joke wasted.

Media Person

Dear *New York Times Magazine*:

After reading your fascinating article on the Proustian scholar who's translating *A la Recherche du Temps Perdu* into English (he hasn't gotten to the title yet but apparently *Remembrance of Things Past* just doesn't cut it anymore) in a way that is scrupulously faithful to the immortal spirit of the monumental masterpiece, Media Person was burning to read the thing. But the guy says it's going to take him *ten years*.

Wouldn't it be easier if we all just learned French?

Media Person

Dear Mark Kostabi:

According to *New York* magazine, you are furious because someone is selling forgeries of your paintings. This raised the question of whether there can be such a thing as a forgery of your paintings since you, as an iconoclastic giant of postmodernist art, have proudly admitted that many of your paintings are in fact painted by assistants. After chewing this thing over, Media Person has decided that yes, there can be a Kostabi forgery. Since the public has come to accept that a Kostabi painting is one *not* painted by Kostabi, then the only fake Kostabi would be one painted by Kostabi.

Therefore, Media Person is sorry to inform you, if you pick up a paintbrush, you're under arrest.

Media Person

Dear NRA:

Guns don't kill people. People don't kill people. People with guns kill people.

Media Person

Dear Liz Smith:

Media Person was watching TV and heard you ask: "Why do talk-show hosts always sit on the right?"

Easy, Liz. Because ours is a right-side-of-the-road culture. In vehicles, the person in control, or driver, sits on the left (TV-screen right). This has become the power position in side-by-side seating arrangements in our society and the host instinctively takes it to establish dominance. In other words, right makes might.*

Media Person

Dear President Bush:

There has been some controversy over your decision to put the space program back into high gear.

As a fellow visionary, Media Person fully supports you.

It is our right, indeed our highest destiny as Americans, to seek out the farthest reaches of the universe, to explore new, uncharted worlds, to find creative new ways to exploit them and extract huge profits from them and ultimately *to screw them up completely*.

Media Person

---

*Know what's great about being an author? You just make up stuff like this and throw it in the book and all of a sudden it looks official, it's on microfilm in the Library of Congress, and people believe it and go on quoting it for years, just like you were saying something intelligent.

Dear Heritage Foundation:

You can make Ed Meese a Distinguished Fellow but that doesn't make him a distinguished fellow.

Media Person

Dear Linda Ellerbee:

Once Media Person would hear the words "Hello, I'm Linda Ellerbee" and expect your wry, albeit slightly precious, take on the news.

Now he cringes. Here comes a sales pitch for Maxwell House coffee. Worse, a sales pitch ineptly disguised as some kind of pseudonewscast. Worst, a sales pitch costarring fatuous, rotund weatherclown Willard Scott.

Media Person was pleasantly surprised when a minor uproar broke out over this, surprised because the stigma against selling out has all but disappeared. So, a betrayal by someone who seemed to have integrity and independence still carries shock value, apparently.

Ellerbee, repent! Renounce the evil plug. Bite Willard's ass and tell us coffee beans are coffee beans. Your soul will feel ten percent creamier—freshens your breath, too!

Media Person

Dear Tom Clancy:

Media Person has a surefire idea for your next novel, which he herewith offers free of charge:

Despite his inability to create a single believable character, a middle-aged military-hardware nut becomes a best-selling author with boys-and-their-toys novels portraying war as a crisp, clean, high-tech game played on computer screens by cool guys. This helps create a climate of soaring military budgets and a new generation of trillion-dollar sci-fi weapons. Finally a nuclear war breaks out and the entire human race dies a nasty but colorful death—except for two astronauts stationed on Mars (one American, one

Russian) and the novelist, who is visiting them on a free VIP tour arranged by the military. Inspired, the novelist starts his next book, about a war between the last two human beings, a Russian and an American. But when the novelist tells the two astronauts his plot, they decide he's a pathologically violent ideologue and kill him.

Pretty ironic, huh?

Media Person

Dear Elie Wiesel:

With due respect for your agonizing question of why a just God would permit the existence of the Nazis, it seems to Media Person the reason is obvious: to provide Hollywood with the ultimate, perfect villains. After all, without Hitler, there would have been no *Casablanca*, *Raiders of the Lost Ark*, or *The Great Dictator*. *Patton* would have been about a colonel in charge of a motor pool in Oklahoma. *The Sound of Music* would have been about a singing family escaping from ski instructors. *The Longest Day* would have been over in five minutes. And who would the bad guys in *Star Wars* have modeled their uniforms after?

Hope this helps.

Media Person

Dear Doctor Surgeon General, Sir:

As your job is overseeing the health of our nation, Media Person feels it is his duty as a citizen to alert you to an alarming symptom of trouble:

Any society in which the term *do-gooder* is an insult is not a healthy society.

Media Person

P.S. Hope the salutation's right.

Dear Media Person:

We get gassed by the Iraqis and bashed by the Turks. But in the West we get ignored. We're a big nationality and we deserve our own country, but no one knows we exist. What do you advise?

The Kurds

Dear Kurds:

You've got to lose that awful name. At best it sounds like something nursery-rhyme characters eat, at worst a cross between *nerd* and *crud*. Here in the West, that doesn't play. Makes you sound like losers.

Go hire yourselves a media consultant pronto. He'll whip up a hot new moniker that will change your image—and your destiny. Something like the People of the Hawk. Are there hawks on your turf? Not that it matters. This will get your top Kurd on the talk shows—hope he has some sex appeal. Next thing you know, rock stars are holding telethons for you, you're all over the slick magazines, and your troubles are over.

Media Person

I'd Gawk a While
at a Tamil

Newspaper editors do not know this and it will hurt them to learn it, but the truth must be told: There are stories no one reads.

Because no one *can*. Certain subjects are so stupefyingly dull or impenetrably alien or forbiddingly unknown that they actually repel the human eyeball and send it skittering down the page crazy out of control till it crashes into a painless bunion removal ad. This is a scientific fact.*

The waste involved in this process is tragic. Reporters write a story, editors edit, printers print, gallons of ink flow . . . and no living brain will ever drink it in.

Ask yourself, for instance, if you have ever read one story about the Tamil rebels of Sri Lanka. If you are honest, you have answered: "Well, er, let's see; of course I have . . . Okay, not really."

Tamils are eyeball-repellent to the average American.

Even among the elite upper classes there are those who believe—

*There are those who feel that the word *media* has this effect on many people, but Media Person cannot permit himself to consider something that depressing.

Media Person has heard them muttering in small knots at polo matches (he hears them on ESPN)—that Tamils are fictional characters invented by the editors of *The New York Times* to help fill the endless sea of news pages in section A. These are devoted to vital dispatches from foreign lands preceded by punchy headlines such as:

UNDER THE HOT DESERT SUN, A YOUNG TRIBESMAN LEARNS
TO REPAIR A DHOW AS HIS ANCESTORS HAVE DONE
SINCE TIME IMMEMORIAL, ONLY NOW WHILE WORKING,
HE LISTENS TO MADONNA ON HIS WALKMAN,
ANOTHER OF THOSE IRONIC CONTRAST THINGS
WE'RE ALWAYS POINTING OUT IN THIS
FASCINATING WORLD WE LIVE IN

The mutterers ask, not unreasonably: "If there really are Tamils, how come there are no Tamil restaurants in our larger cities? And why is it that the only place one ever reads about Tamils is in *The New York Times*? And have we ever seen a Tamil on Phil or Oprah? No. Transsexual Satan worshippers by the score but nary a Tamil."

Of course the Tamils are not fictional. The reason they seem fictional is no fault of theirs but of the U.S. educational system, which neglected to notice that there is such a place as Sri Lanka with a populace divided between dominant Sinhalese and an oppressed Tamil minority. If Americans don't know who Tamils are or where they live, how can Americans be interested in what they're doing, which at the moment seems to be fighting an endless, unnoticed guerrilla war in the back of *The New York Times*?

A much larger war, fought between Iran and Iraq, went on back there for nearly a decade undefiled by American eyeballs.

So does most of what happens in Africa, South America, and the U.S. Congress.

But it's not only subject matter that makes certain things unreadable. Nearly all newspaper editorials, for instance, are unreadable. Go ahead, try to finish one. See? You can't. Editorials should have become extinct years ago. Media Person doesn't get it.

But Media Person cannot be overly concerned about editorials or Tamils or Iraqis or Democrats at the moment because he is too worried about the economy.

It's not that he fears an economic collapse, though some economic experts have predicted one is inevitable. He fears the effect the economic collapse is going to have on the media: There will be nothing in the papers but economic news.

And while Tamil news is unreadable, economic news is incomprehensible. Media Person should know because he reads the economic news every day *even though he can't understand one word of it*.

Neither can anyone else, certainly not the journalists who write it and least of all the economists who instigate it.

What no one except Media Person is willing to admit is that economics makes no sense whatever. Economics is astrology with numbers. It is absolute raving gibberish. It is a swamp that sucks all meaning to a watery death.

You read, for instance, that one of the biggest problems facing the country is its staggering budget deficit. Every financial expert agrees—except those who believe the deficit doesn't matter, those who believe it's actually a good thing, and those who believe there really is no deficit at all; in fact, there's a surplus.

Read a story about the stock market and you learn that most Wall Streeters are bearish—they think the market will drop. You then read that this means the market is sure to rise, because only when Wall Streeters are convinced it must fall can a bull market begin. Therefore, this is an excellent time to invest—except that when the bull market does begin, stock prices will be driven up and the smart money will quickly pull out, causing the market to fall.

Anything you assume is good for us isn't. Take a growing economy with high employment. Sounds healthy, right? Wrong. It causes inflation, which can be devastating. A stronger dollar is good, yes? No. It makes American products more expensive in foreign markets, thus decreasing sales of American exports and worsening our trade deficit.

In fact, any time you think you have even the simplest economic matter figured out—If I have more money, I'm richer, correct? Nope, sorry, wrong, false, forget it, punch yourself in the head six times. It seems inflation, taxes, penalties, and service fees actually have left you penniless, and that's without even factoring in the inverted-yield curve, the wholesale price index, the U.S. Dollar Index, March Futures Contract, and the London Interbank Offered Rate.

Media Person doesn't know if the economy will collapse or not, but his advice is to stock up on plenty of canned goods and old movies. You'll know the crisis is over when the newspapers switch from economics back to English.

The Mad Monk and His Screaming Heads

Media Person liked *The McLaughlin Group* better when Robert Novak was a member.

The man is mad. His eyes smoked. Venom dribbled from his curled lip as he defended the Free World against the communist menace, which could pop up anywhere, especially in the thoughts of a fellow panelist. It was great fun watching Novak hate everyone to the left of Patrick Buchanan. But then he departed and the entertainment level dropped with the advent of his replacement, Patrick Buchanan.

Both are right-wing primitives but also, more interestingly, media split-personality cases. Buchanan is a raving brute in his syndicated newspaper column but on television he's cool, amiable, and low key. Novak is the opposite, an unexciting columnist (he's half of the syndicated Evans & Novak team) but the mad dog of the tube.

Whereas John McLaughlin is a perpetually outraged father who seems to be looking for some errant child to paddle. Everything out of his mouth sounds like a stern admonition, even "Happy Valentine's Day! Bye-bye!"

A Jesuit priest for thirty years, the irritable, sixtyish McLaughlin is the most unlikely person to be host of a successful TV show since Ed Sullivan.

But then *The McLaughlin Group* comes out of Washington, D.C., and much of what goes on there is unlikely. This is a city where individuals chosen at random can not only name the secretary of commerce but actually believe that he does something important. A place where everyone cares passionately who the Democrats nominate for governor of Idaho.

A place where people are so obsessed with politics they will even watch it on television on a Sunday morning.

Of course, the reason politics is on then is that hardly anyone watches television Sunday mornings, most people being either asleep, in church, or both. Since there is no audience, this is the perfect time for our conscientious TV executives to discharge their obligation to provide meaningful public-affairs programming for the American public.*

When it started in 1982, *The McLaughlin Group* was a radical (sorry, McLaughlin) departure. Previously, Sunday-morning political shows were designed with one objective in mind: to achieve perfect dullness. Do Not Rock the Boat was the unstated commandment. They were so dull they appeared to be televised not in color, or even black and white, but in gray.

Most of these shows could be divided into two types: Poke the Pols and Preening Pundits. The former, consisting of efforts like *Bleat the Press* and *Mace the Nation,* in theory had great potential. Here were government officials haled before media inquisitors who had license to snort in derision. *But they didn't.* Overly polite, the questioners too often smiled in the face of sophistries, euphemisms, evasions, and the most preposterous outright lies. What a waste! All those talking heads propped before the cameras and not a pie put in flight.

On Preening Pundit shows, the reporters, many of them lowly toilers in the print mines, climbed into the sunshine and dared to

---

*Washington is so weird *The McLaughlin Group* is shown there on *Saturday night*.

utter their own opinions, though often not very interesting ones. Still, they were enormously grateful for the opportunity as TV exposure could lead to lucrative fees on the lecture circuit.

Despite the many controversies and passions raging through public life, the Preening Pundits strove to keep things calm. In fact, on *Washington Week in Review,* a typical representative of the genre, they generally kept things unconscious.

Here tired, middle-aged white men in glasses would sit around a conference table, play with their pencils, and tell one another what happened in Congress last week until whatever audience existed had passed out. These were nodding heads.

While such shows seemed inspired by study halls at night sessions of Nerd State Junior College, *The McLaughlin Group* must have been conceived with an eye toward the world of pro wrestling.

No restraint here. People attack and interrupt each other, hoot down dubious assertions, hurl insults with abandon, and generally behave as if in a saloon in a gold rush boomtown. Raucous cries of "Baloney!" "Ridiculous!" and "Oh, come on!" ring out. Horselaughs abound. Far from being a calming influence, McLaughlin himself may at any moment leap at an exposed jugular.

"You're getting like him!" he wailed on one occasion. "The two of you are *Gremlins Two.*" Sometimes he makes fun of the others' names, delighting, for instance, in calling Morton Kondracke *Mor-Tonne.*

He also delights in goading his charges into rash predictions and shoot-from-the-lip summations. Indeed, the show is notorious for McLaughlin's attempts to reduce complex issues to glib one-liners. "Exit Question," Media Person expects to hear McLaughlin scream any week now. "On a scale of one to ten, what is the meaning of life?"

So much for the dullness problem. As often happens in human existence, things had swung from one extreme to another. From dreary, must-miss civics lesson, politics on TV had turned into geeks biting the heads off chickens.

Whipped by McLaughlin, the show rattles along furiously. Panelists have learned they must talk very fast and very loud or be shouted down. After rushing through an intro, McLaughlin tosses each topic to the wolves for a quick chew. "Issue one!" he once barked. "Conciliation *sí*, confrontation *no*. Or, Don Regan puts his James Baker uniform on."

What? Who? Dazed by the surge of inside references, some viewers outside the D.C. Beltway pitch over with terminal vertigo. But others get an adrenaline rush as the groupies surround a topic and tear it apart, often finishing it off with all five yelling at once and then the charged-up theme music drowning out the already unintelligible rhetoric. No time for subtleties. On to Gorbachev's new economic policies!

It's amusing to see how quickly newcomers adapt to the *Group* spirit. When Novak was on, within minutes of exposure, hitherto innocent newsies would begin frothing at the mouth and hurling imprecations. Media Person remembers the time Eleanor Clift of *Newsweek*, whom he had previously seen droning responsibly on other shows, turned up. That day McLaughlin was in great anguish that Ronald Reagan had personally betrayed him by retreating before Congress on some tedious matter of great significance to conservatives.

McLaughlin grumbled about appeasement. Novak rushed to defend his president, affecting sorrow for the viewers, "subjected to this baloney you have given them." McLaughlin intimated that Novak was blind. Jack Germond, the show's token liberal, found himself in the uncomfortable position of agreeing with McLaughlin, whom he has called "a master of tortured reasoning." Then Clift piped up with a light jab to the host. "John," she said, "Ronald Reagan's never gonna be the man you want him to be."

"You mean the Rambo of the right?" said McLaughlin. "He won't be that?"

"Maybe," mused Clift, "they took some wrong things out when they operated on him this summer."

There was a moment of stunned silence, followed by someone going, "*Wooo!*"

Even in the fevered atmosphere of *The McLaughlin Group*, that one had brought them up short.

Perhaps because it took the invective in a different direction. The real problem with *The McLaughlin Group*, Media Person realized, was not its rowdiness, which, after all, merely mirrors the increased incivility of society in general over the last few decades. It was that the nasty attitude was misapplied. *The McLaughlin Group* had blundered at the outset. It shouldn't have set up as a Preening Pundit show but a Poke the Pols show. Father McLaughlin and his holy terrors should be terrorizing not each other (who cares about hurting the feelings of journalists?) but the brutes who drive us all crazy—governors, senators, generals, corporate chiefs, popes, and presidents.

The McLaughlin Group is a cheap handgun pointed in the wrong direction.

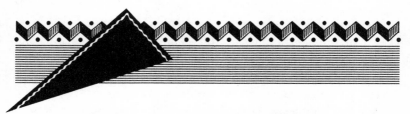

Terror Stalks
the Science Pages

WARNING: Reading this chapter may cause dizziness, headache, nausea, a slight rise in body temperature, and a panicky feeling that your life can be randomly snuffed out at any moment without warning. If these symptoms persist, put the book down and take a long nap.

Media Person won't soon forget the day he was sitting peacefully in his own home, not bothering anyone, when he saw this headline in *The New York Times*:

HUMAN TEETH, ALREADY SMALL, KEEP ON SHRINKING

Good God. Media Person ran his tongue over his teeth and blanched. They *did* feel smaller, but he couldn't be sure. Alarmed, Media Person took a ruler and tried to measure his molars. They seemed stable enough, but he couldn't stop thinking about them and after a while began to worry that his entire head was shrinking. Would he be able to meet his responsibilities—which mainly involve the absorption of large amounts of reading matter—with a skull the size of a walnut?

You'd think that science editors would realize that many readers are suggestible and can be seriously deranged by inflammatory headlines. You'd think they'd try to make the science pages less upsetting. You'd think wrong.

Media Person has often wondered why science news is so aggressive. Why must we always be made to feel that death is imminent, not only our own but also that of the entire planet? Why can't the science and health news leave us in peace?

There isn't a week that goes by without a rash of dire health alarms in the press.

CELERY CAUSES CANCER!

EATING ANIMAL CRACKERS RAISES HEART ATTACK RISK IN BALDING MALES!

All the poor suckers who eat celery or animal crackers feel sudden terror. (Some may have a heart attack induced by the headline itself.) Those who don't are silently congratulating themselves on their wisdom. But next week, the stories are rescinded and new alarms are issued!

CELERY PREVENTS CANCER BUT INCREASES RISK OF STROKE!

MOST HEART ATTACKS CAUSED BY WATCHING TV!

The oat bran blitz of 1989 was typical of the genre. The media started running stories that oat bran prevented heart disease. Previously oats were considered fit only for horses, but now they were magic. America's trendiest people (two-thirds of the populace) charged into the supermarkets screaming for oat bran. Sales boomed. Oat bran mutated into new and varied forms. Soon you expected oat bran wine and oat bran cheese. Then the media literally had a change of heart. Oat bran was repealed. Turned out it wouldn't make your heart healthier after all. It was nothing but . . . food.

In March 1990, *USA Today* ran a story on new findings about carcinogens under a headline that summed up the desperate confusion many readers must have been feeling by now on the whole subject of food and health:

EATING CAUSES CANCER?

Why does this madness keep happening?

After years of constant anxiety, Media Person decided to find out. He did scientific research and discovered what's behind the horror that gnaws at us from within the science pages.

First of all, there are basically four different kinds of science articles found in newspapers, namely:

1. Stories about truly revolutionary scientific discoveries, real breakthroughs so important that afterward human life will never be the same. This kind of story comes along rarely, and when it does, its importance is almost never recognized. The button, for instance. The media completely missed the invention of the button.

2. Stories about discoveries that may or may not become important in the future but are totally incomprehensible except to an MIT doctoral candidate in nuclear biophysics. This is the most common type of science story. It frequently deals with the discovery of particles so tiny that we are assured that nothing smaller can possibly exist. A year later, even tinier ones are discovered.

3. Stories about scientists discovering things that the rest of us either already knew or couldn't care less about. This unamazing-discovery story has proliferated greatly in recent years due to the computer. Increased computer advertising has resulted in much more space to fill in the science section. In fact, before computer ads, there usually *was* no science section. Editors try to fill the space with news of pseudobreakthroughs, especially by social scientists, such as these recent discoveries:

• People hate being criticized, according to research psychologists.
• Children dislike homework.
• Horses like other horses.

- Scientists have discovered how the human sense of smell works: Odors enter the nose, of all organs, waft around the nostrils a bit, and finally are turned into informational impulses that alert the brain.
- To mix a deck of cards thoroughly, researchers have found, it is best to shuffle seven times. Fewer are not enough. More does not significantly improve the mix.

All these wild revelations appeared in long articles in "Science Times," a weekly section in *The New York Times*.

4. The last basic type of science story is the aforementioned scary type that shrinks our teeth and gives us nightmares.

Did you know that between 1983 and 1988, seven U.S. servicemen and relatives were killed by soda vending machines? It seems they like to topple over after being rocked vigorously, crushing the rocker.

Did you know that an average of 8,716 toothpick-related injuries occurred annually in the U.S. between 1979 and 1982? It's a fact, according to the media.

That's the kind of thing Media Person is talking about. Before reading this, you never gave a thought to the dangers of toothpicks or soda machines. Now you can never look at another one without wondering if it's plotting to do you in.

But of course the worst are those disease stories. Media Person's scientific study of science stories revealed that the vast majority of terrifying health articles come from one source: the most dangerous publication in America, *The New England Journal of Medicine*.

Newspapers and wire services constantly lift the most morbid and grisly offerings from this magazine and pass them along to readers. *The New England Journal of Medicine* is the bible of hypochondriacs the world over. They delight in discovering and imagining themselves suffering from diseases such as:

- *Killer Strep:* Once dull little streptococcus bacteria moping around the western U.S. mutate into vicious, homicidal germs with a thirst to kill. One minute you're walking along happy as Vanna White, the next you're writhing on the floor clutching your throat in agony as though the Joker had doctored your mascara.

- *St. Anthony's Fire:* A killer fungus stalking Connecticut which, according to the AP, "makes its victims feel as if they are being roasted alive."
- *The Stendhal Syndrome:* Media Person swears he isn't making this up. Tourists, ordinary tourists on foreign vacations, suddenly have mental breakdowns when visiting culture-drenched places like Florence because, according to *Newsday*, they're "overwhelmed or bewildered by the quantity, quality, and historical significance of what they are seeing."
- *Trichotillomania:* Victims cannot stop themselves from ripping the hair out of their heads as well as from their eyebrows and eyelashes.

Every one of these grotesque diseases Media Person read about in some newspaper and was soon convinced that he had contracted it.

Media Person's scientific analysis also brought to light the motive behind the plague of journalistic terrorism. Science writers and editors—throughout their careers scorned as nerds, relegated to the back of the paper, never getting to feel the thrill of big breaking stories, forced to interview biochemists instead of movie stars—are taking it out on the world, exercising power the only way they can, by scaring the hell out of us.

They sit at their computer screens giggling maniacally as readers all over the city blanch in terror, clutch their chests, and slowly sink to the floor.

Dr. Frankenstein's monster, a much put-upon individual, would understand. This is the revenge of the science editor.

Soon after making this important discovery, Media Person came across an Associated Press story that opened this way:

A long-lost, tree-dwelling relative of humans and apes has been found in a leech-infested rain forest in Madagascar, an event described as one of the most important rediscoveries of mammals in a decade.

Bernhard Meier, a biologist at Ruhr University in Bochum, West Germany, emerged from the forest with an injured knee, blood poisoning and malaria—as well as the first photographs of the hairy-eared dwarf lemur, a tiny primate not seen since 1875.

Now there was Media Person's idea of great science writing. In two sentences, we have a thrilling adventure story rivaling any saga of Indiana Jones. It's entertaining, it's colorful, and, most important, it doesn't threaten you in any way. And something about it—maybe the exotic locale and the creature's hilarious name—gives the piece a Monty Pythonesque touch of the absurd.

But knowing the proclivities of science journalism, Media Person couldn't really enjoy the story. He kept worrying that the next day or the next week he'd have to face something like this:

RARE LEMUR ESCAPES LAB,
DEVOURS POPULACE OF MADAGASCAR,
HEADS FOR U.S.

The Case of
the Livid Legend

BAILIFF: Oyez, hear ye and shaddup! Court is now in session, the honorable Media Person presiding. All rise.

MEDIA PERSON: Be seated. This is Media Court, the only court empowered to condemn people on the basis of what's written about them in the papers. Bailiff, who's on the docket today?

BAILIFF: Your honor, the legendary New York newspaper columnist Jimmy Breslin is charged with committing gross insensitivity in the newsroom.

SPECTATORS: Buzz buzz mutter mutter.

MEDIA PERSON: Order! Order in the court! Anyone causing a disturbance will have sordid details of his sex life fed to the supermarket tabloids. All parties are forthwith warned that this solemn proceeding will be conducted in a fair, impartial, and even-handed manner. Okay, drag in the guilty bastard and let's string him up.

DEFENSE COUNSEL: Objection!

MEDIA PERSON: Bailiff, eject that objector. I know a troublemaker when I see one.

(Brief commotion as the defense counsel is flung bodily from the courtroom.)

PROSECUTOR: I must say, your honor, this is most irregular.

MEDIA PERSON: Chuck him out too, bailiff. The fewer lawyers, the quicker we wrap this thing up and get to lunch.

(Bailiff gives prosecutor the heave-ho.)

MEDIA PERSON: Now, Mr. Breslin, according to the indictment presented by the media, you did, in the office of *New York Newsday* on Friday, May 5, 1990, throw a major tantrum and spew unbelievably vile verbal abuse—sexist, racist, and obscene—at a colleague. How do you plead?

BRESLIN: Aw, jeez, I already apologized for that.

MEDIA PERSON: Clerk, enter a plea of "guilty as hell."

PROSECUTOR (*climbing back in through a window*): Your honor, defendant referred to the reporter, a Korean-American named Ji-Yeon Yuh, as a "yellow cur." According to newspaper accounts, he screamed: "The fucking bitch doesn't know her place. She's a little dog, just a little cur, a cur running along the street. She's a yellow cur." He also referred to the woman as "slant-eyed" and used—I quote *The New York Times*—"a lewd anatomical reference."

MEDIA PERSON: A regular Sir Galahad, isn't he?

DEFENSE COUNSEL (*crashing through the courtroom door*): My client was provoked, your honor.

MEDIA PERSON (*sighing*): Not as much as I am. But, all right, what's his excuse for his inexcusable outburst?

DEFENSE COUNSEL: She attacked his work, your honor, after obtusely misunderstanding it, the work of a fellow employee and a distinguished Pulitzer Prize–winning columnist, a man long recognized as one of America's foremost chroniclers of urban life and a champion of the oppressed.

PROSECUTOR: Untrue, your honor. She legitimately complained about defendant's flagrantly offensive disparagement of the female gender.

MEDIA PERSON: I assume you're referring to Exhibit A, the Breslin column published in *New York Newsday* on Thursday, May 4,

1990, and headlined, "Officially, the Spouse Is Out of the House."

DEFENSE COUNSEL: Correct, your honor. It's a charming, playful account of Mr. Breslin's domestic troubles. As you know, his wife was recently elected a New York City Councilwoman and Mr. Breslin, employing the classic humorous device of the exasperated husband, comically grumbles that Mrs. Breslin's job keeps her from helping him with his wardrobe and other spousal duties.

PROSECUTOR: It's a column that insulted not only his wife, but all women. It was sexist, demeaning, and bilious. Defendant writes, "I hate official women." He wants women kept in their place as they were in the old days of male domination.

BRESLIN: For Christ sake, can't anyone take a joke anymore?

MEDIA PERSON: Try to restrain yourself, Mr. Breslin, or I will have you hurled into a pit of radical feminists. Now what happened after the column appeared?

PROSECUTOR: Ms. Yuh sent a note to Mr. Breslin, as is the right of every American, complaining that it was inappropriate for him to use his column in *Newsday* to insult women. Mr. Breslin's response was to indict an entire race and gender in the most despicable terms. He slandered Ms. Yuh in the presence of several other reporters.

DEFENSE COUNSEL: Hold on. Ms. Yuh did not just complain to my client. She also fired off an officious protest to his boss.

PROSECUTOR: Which is also her right. She, too, works for *Newsday*, and was appalled to see her newspaper printing sexist slurs.

DEFENSE COUNSEL: Your honor, I call to the stand the Murray Kempton column. Mr. Kempton, also a *Newsday* columnist and Pulitzer Prize winner, is a beloved figure in the journalistic community and considered by many the conscience of the profession.

> It is finkery to criticize him to his boss and to sign petitions demanding that all your mutual bosses pick his pocket with a two-week suspension without pay.

MEDIA PERSON: "Finkery"? Strong word. Silly word, too. But Ms. Yuh is not on trial here. She is not famous enough for Media Court to get excited about.

DEFENSE COUNSEL: Your honor, my client's outburst was unfortunate, but he was under stress. Ms. Yuh rattled his cage. We all say things we don't mean in the heat of anger, and Mr. Breslin's temper is famous. As a character witness, I call to the stand Mr. Breslin's wife, the honorable Ronnie Eldridge, or at least a statement Ms. Eldridge issued. Bear in mind that it was she whom Mr. Breslin's column allegedly insulted. She is also, obviously, a woman.

Jimmy is not a sexist . . . He delights in his wife's accomplishments and always supports her efforts.

He is also not a racist. People in need of power have rarely had a more ardent spokesperson. His anger with greed and injustice are what sends him out the next day.

He is an artist. He has written fine books and memorable columns. His view of the world is special and consistent and wonderful.

But he is also outrageous. And he has a quick and miserable temper. He lost it the other day and said terrible and regrettable things. Sadly for him, he found no compassion or forgiveness.

MEDIA PERSON: Isn't blaming his hot temper just a way of trying to evade responsibility for his words?

DEFENSE COUNSEL: Mr. Breslin has apologized for his words.

PROSECUTOR: Sure, under pressure from his boss. He apologized after the editor reprimanded him.

DEFENSE COUNSEL: His apology was sincere.

MEDIA PERSON: Let's hear the apology. Clerk, if you please.

I am no good and once again I can prove it. I intended to make noise, not offend nice people. I am sorry. I said things I shouldn't have said. The racial and sexual insults I spewed are never appropriate. Again, I am sorry.

PROSECUTOR: He wasn't sorry for long. Because shortly thereafter, he called a notorious radio comedy show and made a mockery of his own so-called apology. He joked about the incident with radio personality Howard Stern and stated that all his apologies are carbon copies of each other. It was only then that *Newsday* suspended him, for his obvious callousness and insensitivity to the whole issue, which was terribly painful to Ms. Yuh and the other Asian-Americans who work at *Newsday*. Previously the editors had resisted their demands for suspension and insisted that Breslin's apology was sincere.

MEDIA PERSON: Howard Stern, the shock jock? The jeering vulgarian who's made a career out of impersonating a twelve-year-old boy desperate to outrage his parents? The jerk who goads blabber-prone celebrities to even greater gaffes? Don't tell me you're going to call him as a character witness.

DEFENSE COUNSEL: No, your honor.

MEDIA PERSON: Good, because Media Person is trying to avoid capital punishment this year.

DEFENSE COUNSEL: What needs to be understood, your honor, is that Mr. Breslin's rage is an integral part of his greatness. Without it, he would not be able to function as a columnist. He erupts with rage over the inequities and iniquities of our society. He is perpetually mad. It is his genius.

MEDIA PERSON: Is defense counsel leading up to an insanity plea?

PROSECUTOR: Just because the man is a professional maniac does not make him crazy.

DEFENSE COUNSEL: No, we're basing our case on the First Amendment, your honor.

BAILIFF: All genuflect to the First Amendment!

(*A moment of religious silence falls over the courtroom as everyone gets down on his or her knees.*)

MEDIA PERSON: Well, you've said the magic words, counselor. If there's any religion here in Media Court, it's the First Amendment. Why didn't you tell me sooner? We could've all been home by now watching *America's Dirtiest Home Videos*.

PROSECUTOR: I protest, your honor. This is not a First Amendment issue. No government restraint is involved or any other form of censorship. After all, *Newsday* printed the offensive column about Breslin's wife.

DEFENSE COUNSEL: But then *Newsday* silenced him for two weeks. His readers were deprived of his voice. Isn't that a form of censorship?

PROSECUTOR: Twaddle. He never takes vacations? This is nothing more than an employee-relations issue. A simple case of racial and sexual harassment. Defendant was properly punished by his employer for his barbaric behavior toward another employee.

DEFENSE COUNSEL: Ms. Yuh was not even present during Mr. Breslin's unfortunate remarks.

PROSECUTOR: Other people were. She heard about them very quickly. As a highly paid, highly visible representative of *Newsday*, Breslin has a responsibility to behave like a decent human being in public. He didn't, so he had to pay the price. And not a very stiff price at that. Many people think he deserved to be fired.

DEFENSE COUNSEL: Defendant was punished for nonconformity. He was ambushed by a bunch of pressure groups. Today everyone is organized into posses. Say the wrong thing and they lynch you. Andy Rooney is suspended by CBS for being exactly the cranky curmudgeon CBS pays him to be. Jimmy the Greek is fired for an off-the-cuff remark in an interview. A Florida sheriff prosecutes a rap group that sells millions of records. Acclaimed artists lose their funding after an outcry by the bluenoses. Speakers are shouted down on college campuses. If someone dislikes a TV show he organizes a sponsor boycott. This case is about an embattled individual versus the censoring mob. *Newsday*'s editors are not really concerned with Jimmy Breslin's sensitivity. They're just hypocrites terrified of petitions and boycotts and pressure groups. This is the danger to free speech today. If our strongest voices are squelched, soon we'll all sound alike. People will censor themselves rather than risk this kind of humiliation and punishment. There will be no more real writers heard in the land, just the voice of the committee.

BAILIFF: All rise!

(*Total confusion. Media Person rushes into the courtroom, sandwich in hand.*)

MEDIA PERSON: Sorry, I just quietly slipped out for a snack during those boring speeches. Be seated, folks. I will now render my verdict, which I chewed over for some time—literally. First, I'm surely not happy about the specter of Sensitivity Police running around bopping anyone who says anything that anyone else in America finds offensive, but I can't acquit the defendant just because of an ugly climate. Cases of this kind tend to be complicated and must be considered individually. One thing all reasonable people can agree on is that Breslin's behavior was disgusting. But the question is, should it be punished? If this brouhaha had taken place in some normal kind of office, if Breslin wasn't a famous columnist but an insurance claims adjuster or a fortune-cookie inspector, and blew up at a coworker, calling her names a dog shouldn't have to hear, spewing racial hate and obscenity around the office, wouldn't his boss be justified in disciplining him? An outburst this virulent and degrading crosses the line of speech; at best it's a breach of civility and decorum, at worst, a virtual assault. It's not an expression of ideas but an explosion of hatred. The argument that it was only a single unfortunate outburst and not a pattern is undermined by Breslin's further provocations on the Stern broadcast. Now I would love nothing more than to issue a ringing defense of my favorite amendment, the First. Had it been the government or some outside power trying to bust Breslin, by God, I'd rise majestically and smite the censors down! Had it been something he wrote in his column that got him suspended, I'd be all over those management bums. Hey, I'll allow any utterance of ideas, no matter how obnoxious or obscene or abstractly symbolic—that's the kind of guy I am—but I'm damned if I'll invoke the Fabulous First to protect a *tantrum*. When some slob in the bleachers pours beer on somebody, he deserves to be tossed out of the park. Breslin poured bile. This court upholds the suspension and sentences the defendant's mouth to be washed out with soap. Will the charwoman please escort the prisoner to the laundry room and execute punishment. As for me, I'm outta here. It's naptime. Oh, one other thing: Mr. Prosecutor, Don't ever say the word *twaddle* in my courtroom again.

(*Media Person bows, then rushes off, pausing briefly to sign auto-graphs. Canned music and applause are heard.*)

BAILIFF: All rise. It's a wrap. Court adjourned. Film at eleven. Good night, Chet. Good night, David. This court made possible by a grant from the Chubb Corporation. Good night and good luck. Write if you get work. Address all appeals to Judge Wapner of *The People's Court,* the only higher authority than this tribunal. Nighty-night, everyone.

Forward to Nowhere

Examining the significant new macro-trends (as he often does when he can't fall asleep), Media Person saw a *Time* cover story that said the U.S. is bogging down in perpetual gridlock: Nothing can move on the ground or in the air. The country is snarled to a standstill.

But then Media Person read a story in *Vanity Fair* that said everything in America is speeding up. According to the writer, Tony Schwartz, everyone is running and doing and getting so fast that life has become a perpetual sprint. He called this "the acceleration syndrome."

Well, whoa! Which trend do ya trust?

After several seconds of deep, probing thought, Media Person realized that both magazines were half right.

The real problem is that the world is speeding up and bogging down at the same time. People are running faster and faster but ending up where they started. The world spins its wheels but goes nowhere.

To make it official, Media Person gave the trend a fancy name: Entropy Acceleration.

It's Entropy Acceleration that accounts for that annoying feeling Media Person gets so often that an awful lot is going on but none of it means anything, those strange, dissonant days when the media are ajangle with news yet somehow it seems like a slow newsday.

The autumn when Media Person discovered Entropy Acceleration, a host of major fall media events—Miss America Pageant, Jerry Lewis Telethon, presidential election campaign, America's Cup, U.S. Open, Olympics—were hurtling toward him in a clamorous rush.

Wow, thought Media Person. They're hot, they're exciting, they're vital, they're spectacular . . . they're gone, they're forgotten, they were meaningless, who cared? Entropy Acceleration.

At the time, one of the great examples of the syndrome was Ed Koch, the most popular of New York's despised mayors. Every day Koch made headlines. He proposed a new foreign legion for criminals. He went to court and argued with a judge. He denounced Jesse Jackson. He made up with Jesse Jackson. He accosted bums in the park. He invented a portable toilet for horses. He got booed at a parade. He wrote ringing letters to newspapers. He coauthored a book with John Cardinal O'Connor. He was everywhere, a furious blur of action and purpose.

Meanwhile Calcutta-on-the-Hudson sank ever further into terminal chaos and disrepair. A few months later, Koch was forcibly retired as mayor.

If Nero lived today, he wouldn't fiddle while Rome burns. He'd listen to music on stereo headphones while working out in the gym between holding a press conference/photo op, dedicating a new fire truck, giving a major speech on fire prevention, taking forty-six phone calls, cohosting a talk show, signing a book contract, and sneaking in a power breakfast with the Roman Senate to discuss conflagration policy.

And Rome would burn down faster than it did before.

Hard News
Made Easy

Anyone can carp about the media and their biased, sensational, inaccurate—and let's not forget stupid—coverage of current events. But Media Person isn't just another Monday morning quarterback. He's not afraid to cover the news himself, demonstrating that if care is taken, it can be done in an intelligent, subjective, self-indulgent, joky fashion with plenty of opinions and a minimum of facts, which are boring. What's more, Media Person does it *without ever leaving his apartment*, a feat Woodward and Bernstein would not dare attempt, or even Houdini.

Here, then, are some of Media Person's best-loved news dispatches from the past seventy-five years:

BERLIN WALL TORN DOWN

BERLIN—It seemed wonderfully apropos of the Greedball '80s that in one of the decade's greatest political upheavals, the deepest impulse of the mob was not to liberate a notorious prison or storm a palace but to go *shopping*.

There it was on television: The Berlin Wall gave way to the Berlin Mall.

Will future generations of students someday memorize the date of the Run on Bananas as they now study the Bastille and the Boston Tea Party?

Many American commentators were depressed by the failure of President Bush to capture the occasion with a catchy phrase or memorable gesture. While the presidency has devolved into a public-relations job and Americans no longer really expect their presidents to do much, we do feel entitled to an eloquent gesture now and then. We want a leader who can symbolize and inspire.

So what happens when the White House is occupied by a sym-bolton?

VOYAGER SENDS PHOTOS FROM SPACE

SOMEWHERE IN THE SOLAR SYSTEM—Media Person watched the TV show beamed from Neptune, though in truth Pluto has always intrigued him more. Probably the Disney influence. Besides, Neptune is greedy. We get one lousy moon and Neptune has eight. Is this fair? What's more, one of them is pink, we now learn, with exotic ices and possibly even electric nitrogen winds. Wow. Imagine a couple of Neptunian lovers gazing heavenward on a romantic moonlit night—they could go blind. But we have to make do with a pile of boring gray rocks. Makes you ashamed to admit you're an Earthling, doesn't it?

SCORES INJURED AT KHOMEINI RITES

TEHRAN—Those Iranians really know how to put on a funeral.

It's the kind of send-off Media Person would like when his turn comes: two or three hundred thousand shrieking, grief-crazed readers out in the street rioting, rhythmically beating themselves on the head, rending their garments, and chanting, "Take me with you, O Fabulous One."

Knocking Media Person's body out of the casket and crushing hundreds of mourners is optional.

Maybe that's a bit excessive. Truth is, Media Person would settle for simple cremation with his ashes poured into the ink used to print *The New York Times*. This would be a form of immortality. You'd never get Media Person off your hands.

BUSH REACHES PLATEAU

WASHINGTON—Following venerable tradition, the press dutifully assessed the first hundred days of the Bush administration. The consensus: He is doing fine.

Of course, the evaluation is subject to immediate change in the event that Bush actually does something.

PLANE CRASHES ON LONG ISLAND

NEW YORK—After experts determined that the crash of an Avianca airliner that ran out of fuel in midair was caused by lack of communication between pilot and air traffic controllers, federal safety officials have mandated that flight crews must be trained in the proper use of standard international emergency terminology. This includes phrases such as OMIGOD! WE'RE OUTTA GAS!, HEY! WAKE UP IN THAT TOWER, YOU JERKS!, WE'RE GOING DOWN!, and EEAAAGGGHHHHHHH!!!

LUCY DIES

HOLLYWOOD—Lucille Ball did not die in vain, for she inspired one of those classic *New York Times* headlines that perfectly capture a person's essence in one pithy phrase.

Since the average *Times* reader could not be expected to recognize the comedian's name, the newspaper of record, in its inimitable style, provided identification: "Lucille Ball, Spirited Doyenne of TV Comedies, Dies at 77."

Does that sum up that zany redhead, or what?

As though it were yesterday, Media Person could see an exasperated Desi Arnaz shaking his head and remonstrating in his fractured Cuban accent, "Now Lucy, you got some 'splainin' to do, you darn little spirited doyenne, you."

NEW GROUP FIGHTS RUDENESS

NEW YORK—Media Person salutes the newly formed New York Pride for its crusade against the ill-mannered slobs who are ruining the Big Apple. You know, if we can just get New Yorkers to start using words like *please*, *thank you*, and *excuse me* before they shoot or kidnap someone, this city will be a darn sight more livable for all of us.

COMBATING THE OILY MENACE

WASHINGTON—The Bush administration has found the solution to one of the nation's worst environmental problems, oil spills. Beginning in the fall, supertankers will be required to wear gigantic condoms now being developed by scientists at Uniroyal. Fitting completely over the ship's hull, the new device will enable oil companies to practice safe slicks.

COLD WAR ENDS

BRUSSELS—Now that the Cold War is over and NATO is being converted into a jeep- and tank-rental agency and Serious Rethinking is under way, could everyone in the world please go back to calling military stuff by its proper name? Somewhere along the line, the War Department become "the Defense Department" and money for guns and ammo became "defense spending."

This always made Media Person wonder: How can war still be possible when no nation in the world practices anything but defense? How could anyone commit offense? Let's not just de-militarize, let's de-euphemize.

SOVIET SUB SINKS

SOMEWHERE IN THE NORTH ATLANTIC—What's the problem? Submarines are *supposed* to sink. If it doesn't sink, *then* send out emergency bulletins. Otherwise don't bother us.

IMELDA ARRAIGNED

NEW YORK—Imelda Marcos, widow of Philippines dictator Ferdinand Marcos, arrived in New York to be formally charged with robbing her country blind and of course the press behaved with its customary dignified restraint, impersonating a pack of rabid dingos spotting a wounded wombat.

As the famed shoe collector tried to slip into the Waldorf,

according to the *Daily News*, "about 100 members of the press charged headlong to block her. After about 30 seconds of snarling, grunting and shouting, a path was opened."

For her part, Imelda tried to make the best of her assets and elevate her famous bad taste into neologistic immortality. Asked about her tendency to excess in shoes and life in general, Imelda told her pal, gossip columnist Cindy Adams, "They will list my name in the dictionary some day. They will use 'Imeldific' to mean ostentatious extravagance."

Not necessarily, Media Person is afraid. She'll have to beat out *Liberaceous*, *Trumpatetic*, and *Nancyreaganian*.

VIOLENCE ERUPTS BELOW THE SEA

SEA WORLD, FLA.—Tragedy struck the marine mammal community when a killer whale at Sea World with no known criminal record fatally mugged another killer whale. Media Person believes that the root cause of the orcacide was the late-night talk show *Later* with Bob Costas, which, a few nights before, had shown horrifying footage of Hugh Downs riding orca-back, a humiliation that would derange any creature with a shred of dignity.

ECONOMIC PROBLEMS BEDEVIL U.S.

WASHINGTON—Pennies have become scorned and worthless, economic experts say. No one wants them anymore. At the same time, the dollar bill wears out too easily and many feel a dollar coin is needed.

This one's easy, says Media Person. The government just declares pennies are now worth a dollar.

MISS AMERICA CROWNED

ATLANTIC CITY—Media Person thought the best part of the ever-fascinating pageant was Phyllis George asking the Question Designed to Show That Contestants Are Serious, Intelligent Human Beings, Not Just Bimbos in Bathing Suits.

In response, each contestant would say something like: "I think it's really important for the handicapped to be able to live in a pollution-free environment where no minority group is oppressed by lack of educational opportunity and everyone is free to belong to the religious denomination of his or her choice." She would then smile, turn, and show the judges her tush.

ROMANIA STRUGGLES

BUCHAREST—Following the revolution that deposed the dictator Ceauçescu, Romania was having trouble getting democracy straight, due to inexperience.

In one poignant instance, a Romanian journalist asked the new ruling council how she was supposed to handle the ugly news from China (some massacre or other) as there was now a lack of guidance from the government on what to write.

This shot Media Person back many years to a freshman journalism class in an upstate university where distinguished guest lecturers would never arrive on schedule because of the blizzards blocking the Thruway. Instead, the dean of the journalism school would trudge to the lectern and give his well-rehearsed talk on the People's Right to Know.*

Eureka, Media Person thought. In Romania, the people don't know they have the Right to Know. What an opportunity for our neglected and ignored academics! What should be ordered immediately is an airdrop of five hundred U.S. journalism deans into Romania. They will begin lecturing at a thousand feet and continue until every last Romanian understands the implications of the John Peter Zenger case† and insist on his or her right to a free, vital press filled with garish headlines, cheesecake photos, two full pages of comics, and late scores from the coast.

---

*The class usually responded by asserting the People's Right to Nap.

†A case that is so well known to Americans because of its importance in establishing freedom of the press that there is obviously no need for Media Person to explain it here.

Hold That Tragedy—
We're in a
Commercial

Media Person was annoyed. He was trying to watch *L.A. Law* but the network kept breaking in with bulletins about some stupid plane crash.

L.A. Law had a good story line that night. This young driver kills a kid on a bike, knocking him off the road into some bushes. There are no witnesses. The young man tells his lawyer about it and no one else. The victim is missing, his parents are beside themselves, and the story's all over the news, but the lawyer can't go to the cops because of the attorney-client privilege.

Whereas the plane crash was boring. There were no rich, gory details as reporters had not yet reached the scene.

"What's happening to your values, man?" screamed the news person inside Media Person. "Have you turned into one of those cretins who used to complain when the Watergate hearings preempted their soap operas?"

"But these dumb bulletins just keep repeating the same non-story," whined the entertainment person in Media Person. "They don't even know if there are any injuries. Besides, plane-crash fans can switch over to CNN or any of the three channels now in the midst of their 10 P.M. newscasts, and furthermore, in twenty-five minutes, *L.A. Law* will be over and the eleven o'clock news will be on this station with all the late crash results. I mean, my God, does *any* news, no matter how sketchy, take precedence over *all* entertainment? Is this not Show-Biz America, where the show must go on? And on and on and on?"

Under stress, Media Person was breaking down into his component parts. And Entertainment Person, though getting a bit shrill, seemed to have the upper hand: *L.A. Law* remained onscreen.

"Moreover," Entertainment Person continued, "plane-crash stories on TV are all the same. A bunch of newsies crawling over the site trying hard to suppress that giveaway quiver in the voice and that wild gleam of the eye that betray their all-too-obvious excitement. Listen to them lovingly intone the shamelessly overused *tragedy* and *tragic*. Listen to them marvel as they discover, as if for the first time, the vast, miraculous, cosmic irony that in accidents, some people live and others die. I say they're rubbernecking and I say the hell with them."

"Could you possibly . . ." said News Person but there was no stopping Entertainment Person.

"Even if there is something interesting about the crash, such as the possibility that the plane was blown up by terrorists, then the media usually fail to investigate properly anyway, as you recently forced me to read in the *Columbia Journalism Review*, which I personally find less illuminating than *People*."

"Would you shut up?" News Person shouted. "I can't hear *L.A. Law*."

At that point *L.A. Law* ended and the news came charging in with a trumpet blast of great purpose and self-importance.

Unfortunately there still wasn't much info beyond the first bulletins, so the anchor, Chuck Scarborough, had to vamp.

Then something interesting happened. Viewers started calling up Scarborough on the air. First was an NBC engineer who was home operating his ham radio and had heard some reports on what hospitals the injured were being taken to. Then ordinary citizens from the Long Island neighborhood where the plane had gone down were calling with eyewitness reports. Media Person zapped around and saw the same thing was happening on other channels. It was like a news posse forming out there.

You'd see the anchor hold up a map to show where the crash occurred and hear a caller say, "Move the pen a little lower . . . There! That's it."

It was one of those magic, spontaneous, live-TV phenomena that happen from time to time. The tube unexpectedly awakens from its routine commercial existence and stuns you with a raw, crackling vision of what it might be.

Media Person sat up straight. Next, he figured, the studio phone would chirp and a voice would say, "Chuck? This is Bob the paramedic in an ambulance racing to North Shore Hospital. One of the survivors seems to have regained consciousness. Just a sec, I'll put him on."

Then a hysterical air traffic controller would call and say, "Chuck, it wasn't my fault, I swear to God. The blip just disappeared off my damn radar."

Then: "Chuck, this is the pilot. I'm trapped in the cockpit and this whole thing's gonna blow any second. If my wife is listening, I love you, honey."

Why was this happening? Why were these civilians playing reporter? Maybe, Media Person thought, because after watching a genial anchorguy like Scarborough for decades, they feel they know him personally. They identify. Their pal Chuckie is in trouble! He's got a big story on his hands and no script. It's up to them to help.

No, Media Person thought. It's more than that. It's the McLuhan global-village syndrome. When big stories break live, we all get reconnected. Suddenly, there in our separate modules, we're all neighbors again. And we're caught up in humankind's two deepest and most thrilling impulses, to find out what the hell is going on or, alternatively, having some inside dope, to spill your guts and blab it to the world. Television can play to those needs in a way newspapers never could.

Television has all the luck.

Suddenly Media Person realized that the implications here were enormous. Years and years of Donahue and Oprah and call-in radio shows and TV game shows had turned the American public into active media participants. Now they were further evolving into amateur reporters.

Was this the future of journalism? Maybe as the distinction between reporter and source fades, news organizations won't need professionals anymore. In the future, *everyone* will be a reporter.

"Dan, this is Colonel Baghart with the Eighty-second Airborne. The White House hasn't made the official announcement yet but we just landed in Honduras—or some damn banana republic— and we're taking heavy incoming on our left flank. You think I oughta attack or wait for an air strike?"

"Tom, I can't talk long because I hear sirens but me and the boys just grabbed two million six hundred ninety-three thousand bucks from the Bank of America. I think it's a record, but better check. I despise inaccuracy."

Eventually you won't even need a phone. There will be a TV news booth on every corner, like bank cash machines. You'll just pop the cassette out of your videocam—which you carry with you everywhere—and deposit it in the slot and then stand there and watch it air while you and Chuck provide voiceover banter. From any city in the world.

"Hi, Ted, Raisa Gorbachev again. Well, I think we've quelled the revolt in the Ukraine but now the Moldavians are rioting. Oops, here's Mikhail; looks like he's needing a drink. Gotta run. Catch you later."

Next will come the day when we all have audio-video implants in our brains for instant live hookup to twenty-four-hour-a-day Interactive Anchor Central.

"Peter, I'm fading back to pass but I can't find any receivers. Damn, the Super Bowl's on the line. I'm running, Peter; I see daylight!"

"That's what he thinks, Pete. I'm gonna blindside the egotistical bastard. Watch this!"

The handwriting is on the screen. Professional journalists are a dying breed, Media Person fears. The day of the correspondent is done. The future belongs to the citizen-reporter. The future is clear: News R Us.

Triumph
of the Wheel

The first time Media Person happened upon *Wheel of Fortune*, he thought it was a vapid piece of fluff that could appeal only to a few brain-dead zombies.

Fortunately the press soon set him straight.

The Washington Post said *Wheel* was viewed by forty-two million people every day.

Time said *Wheel* was the highest-rated syndicated series in television history.

The New York Times said *Wheel* was so popular it had become a dominant factor in TV scheduling, sometimes wreaking havoc with local and network news.

People said that Vanna White had blond hair, weighed 107 pounds, measured 36-23-33, and adored greasy White Castle hamburgers. *People* knows what is *really* important.

Thanks to *Wheel of Fortune*, Vanna had become the first person in world history to achieve renown as a professional letter turner. Everyone knew Vanna White. The media alternately fawned over her and sneered at her, and the public was enthralled once again by that fascinating phenomenon, the star with no talent. Vanna was the '80s incarnation of the classic dumb blonde, this time literally, because she was permitted to say little more than a cheery "bye" at sign-off.

But despite all the yammer devoted to Vanna and *Wheel of Fortune*, the press failed to tell Media Person the one thing he yearned to know about this deeply significant yet incredibly stupid national phenomenon: *Why?*

Why had a silly game show that seemed bland as puréed cauliflower dipped in warm milk so captivated the mightiest nation on earth?

No one had a clue. Pat Sajak, the Man Who Introduces Vanna (and whose lesser duties include acting as master of ceremonies) had confessed: "I swear on the grave of every game show host who ever lived that I have no idea."

Thus, much to his distaste, Media Person was forced to turn investigative reporter and conduct a major inquiry. This required two lengthy and unpleasant undertakings:

1. Watching the show again.
2. Thinking about it a lot.

Media Person made the sacrifice. He did this in support of the People's Right to Know. (If you are in that particular group, you should be deeply grateful.)

The shocking truth unearthed by Media Person's investigation can be summed up in one not very exciting but significant word which, if seen on Vanna White's magic letterboard might look like this: VI__ARI__US__ESS.

Media Person will now explain the deep mystery.

Wheel of Fortune was dreamed up by Merv Griffin, the man who spent more than two decades on television demonstrating what Johnny Carson would be like without jokes. Offscreen, Griffin was a successful producer of TV shows and a lifelong puzzle junkie. Whether through conscious design or sheer luck, Griffin worked V__C__RIO__SN____S into every element of *Wheel of Fortune*. The viewer was slipped into the picture, subtly encouraged to imagine himself as a contestant, and swept along in a happy haze of fantasy fulfillment.

Observe the VI__A__IOU__ __E__ __ technique in action, step by fiendishly clever step:

The Players: The job of a *Wheel of Fortune* contestant is basically to melt into the background, so ordinary, standard-issue, interchangeable humanoids are chosen. They're not data-spouting brains like the felonious contestants of the scandalous '50s quiz shows. They don't dress as yams and squeal and wet themselves like those of the whoopie-cushion '70s. The low profiles on *Wheel* get a very brief introduction, then virtually disappear as the camera moves onto the game itself. With the contestants deemphasized, the viewer is free to put himself in their place and play away.

The Game: Two different games are played on *Wheel*. One depends on luck, the other on skill—but not much. Both games are easy enough so that even children can succeed. Not even the most insecure and doltish viewers are frightened off to another channel.

One game, unsurprisingly, is a big, flashy, hypnotic, multicolored carnival wheel that the players use to accumulate an account for "buying" prizes. Only two of the wheel's many wedges (BANKRUPT and LOSE A TURN) contain bad tidings. Most spins land the marker on a dollar amount. Nice odds. The wheel twirls and Mr. and Mrs. VICARI__ __ __ __ __ __SS, playing at home, feel like winners already. It's a feel-good gimmick that helps build the can't-lose aura long used to lure suckers into casinos, shell games, and TV game shows.

Between spins, the contestants take whacks at the other game, a simple spelling puzzle familiar to nonathletic children (at least in Media Person's day) as "Hangman." With a whole family watching, someone at home is bound to guess the mystery phrase before a contestant. The viewers' master-of-the-universe glow further brightens. They're on a roll!

The Cast: Pat and Vanna, the young, cleancut TV version of the oldtime carnival barker and shill, welcome you to the tent. The low-keyed Pat is today's kind of nonauthoritarian authority figure, the forgiving sitcom father, boyishly benign and likable. Any residual doubts or guilt you have about wasting your time on this banal little festival of greed are dispelled by his amiably irreverent banter. And Vanna? In the rush to praise her exquisite letter-turning, what is often overlooked is her other task on the show—*clapping*. She claps constantly, impartially rooting the contestants on. (After all these years, Vanna must have the most powerful palms in America.) Despite her glitzy outfits, which sophisticates deride as tacky but many viewers find glamorous, she's a throwback to the kind of simple, sunny, apple-pie-sexy, all-American girl next door who's content to stay on the sidelines cheering for others. And that's her basic function. She is your own personal cheerleader, subliminally encouraging you to play the game.

The Payoff: As the big wheel whirls, the contestants, and by VI___ ___IOUS extension, the home viewers, are awarded (another ingenious touch, here) *credit*. Credit to be spent later. Wasn't credit what the '80s were really all about? America went on a binge, happily spending borrowed money.

Meanwhile, the contestants have also been guessing at letters in the word puzzle and watching them appear on the board, courtesy of Vanna. The blank mystery phrase is gradually filling in. At home, you're yelling out the answer—usually it's something as simple and banal as "walking on air" or "curiosity killed the cat"—and finally, a contestant gets it and wins the round. So what's your prize? Why, shopping. *You get to go shopping*.

Oh, the sheer, mad brilliance of it. As the Great Merv himself once put it, "It's like being let loose on Rodeo Drive." The winner goes shopping, and so do you, because the focus is on the goods, not the contestant. The camera lovingly roams that stage piled high with "fantastic prizes, fabulous and exciting merchandise," as the announcer always describes them. Consumer heaven! It's as though you can reach out and fondle the VCR, the Isuzu pickup, the Tahitian vacation package for two, and the exquisite ceramic Dalmatian without which no home would be complete. You have been enticed to wallow in two of the most seductive ambiances known to mankind: the feverish excitement of the casino and the primal pull of the department store.

And you have triumphed. There you are at the pinnacle of '80s ecstasy. Maybe you couldn't afford to buy a savings-and-loan association or pull a hostile corporate takeover or manipulate the junk-bond market. But through the miracle of V__C__R__O__S television, you can still jump into the national buying binge. You've been sucked through your screen into that dazzling dreamscape, that NirVanna where you are rescued from being some sullen, hapless, anonymous, noncelebrity nobody from nowhere and transformed into a winner, the only identity worth having in Show-Biz America. For a few minutes, at least, you can feel like a somebody, one of those people with wealth, luck, shiny expensive toys, high-priced clothes, glamour, and fun. Someone, in short, who finally exists.

You know, a big wheel.

Media to N.Y.:
Drop Dead

What a beautiful day it was.

Spring, time of rebirth and renewal!

Birds were singing and skies were sunny. Brooding in his rancid, squalid hovel, Media Person could no longer resist. He decided to rejoin humanity. So he got out his binoculars and peered at the people frolicking outside. This was as close as he wished to come.

The humans looked happy. Many had hopeful, goofy smiles on their faces as if they trusted the tentative signals being sent by nature that winter might really be gone.

"The poor devils," Media Person muttered. "They haven't got a chance."

They didn't know that New York was dead. *The New Republic* had said so. "NYC, RIP," it declared. How embarrassing. New York had died and Media Person had to learn about it from foreigners, neoliberals (whatever they are) from Washington. Where was the vaunted *New York Times*? Where was *New York* the magazine? Actually, Media Person knew the answer to that one. *New York* the magazine was so busy celebrating its twentieth

anniversary (four separate issues were necessary to properly com-
memorate itself) that it never even noticed that New York the city
had dropped dead.

The closest it came was a Pete Hamill article that reeled off most
of the *New York* atrocities cited in *The New Republic*'s death
notice (crime, drugs, AIDS, homelessness, racial conflict, declin-
ing schools and hospitals, rotting infrastructure, terrifying real-
estate prices). But Hamill's conclusion was much different from
The New Republic's. Not only did he manage what is called in the
media a note of cautious optimism, he actually proclaimed New
York "the capital of the modern world."

His basis for positive thinking? "The problems are ferocious,"
Hamill admitted. "Given the history of the past twenty years, one
feels they will be solved for a very simple reason: They must."

Well, it's very simple, all right, but more a wish than a reason.

Just a couple of months after its anniversary jolliness, *New York*
came down out of the clouds long enough to acknowledge that if
it wasn't terrified, others were. In an article headlined "Nervous
About the Nineties," the magazine allowed that the town was
gripped by foreboding and pessimism. People were sullen, frightened, and filled with a sense of hopelessness and impending apoca-
lypse.

This attitude was turning up in other local media. While no
publication went as far as *The New Republic* and published an
obituary for the big burg on the two fetid rivers, despair over the
state of the city became evident.

A whole new kind of article—Media Person thought of it as the
I'm-Outta-Here piece—began appearing in magazines and newspapers with increasing frequency. It was by or about people so fed
up with New York that they were actually abandoning the putrid
sinkhole.

Typical of the genre was a March 1990 op-ed piece in the *Times*.
Under the headline "You Take Manhattan; I'm Gone," semifa-
mous media dabbler Barbara Howar said she had packed up and
moved back to her native North Carolina after a thirty-year ab-

sence. Her personal catalogue of New York horrors, presented as typical, included outrageous rents, the burglary of her home, "the body of my daughter's college classmate . . . found in a green garbage bag," and a taxi ride shared with Tom Wolfe* during which, "apparently enraged by Mr. Wolfe's impeccable white suit, coat and hat, the cabbie careened off into the night, cursing in a foreign tongue as I clung to the frayed strap in the rear seat."

One local columnist, Bill Reel, made I'm-Outta-Here pieces a standard part of his repertoire. Reel's beat on the *Daily News* is working- and middle-class Catholic non-Manhattanites, the kind of native, salt-of-the-earth, neighborhood Noo Yawkuhs who had long been the *News*'s loyal readership before the paper gentrified in a futile attempt to seduce upscale advertisers. Now, in Reel's columns, one found these Flatbush and Flushing Joads lashing Granny atop the old Nissan and decamping for locales as exotic as Florida and New Jersey.

"Bill and Karen, friends of mine, were packing yesterday," a typical Reel effort would begin, and Media Person didn't have to read any further; he knew the rest. Bad schools, no affordable housing, crime and grime, drugs, taxes and corruption, on and on into the deepening night.

In no other columnist Media Person read (and he reads them all) had such defeatist tendencies yet taken root. But occasionally one or another would issue a piercing scream of despair.

After relating a depressing day spent inspecting the city, *New York Newsday*'s Denis Hamill flatly said: "I think from just walking around yesterday with my eyes and ears open that the city has finally died and those of us who remain are just pallbearers." Hamill didn't mention whether he'd convinced his brother of this conclusion or whether Pete still believed the city's problems would be solved because they must be solved.

Things reached such a state that David Dinkins, who replaced Ed Koch as mayor in 1990 and was immediately forced to make

---

*Wolfe, of course, would write a famous novel (*The Bonfire of the Vanities*) which portrayed New York as, if not dead, amazingly screwed up.

deep budget cuts in already ravaged vital services—hospitals, schools, police—had to publicly deny that the end was near.

"I can tell you New York is not the *Titanic*," he informed reporters.

This remark occasioned a sarcastic cartoon in the *Post* showing Dinkins underwater on the deck of a sunken ship labeled "*NY*," repeating his message to a fish.

Months later, with ever more bullets in the air, Dinkins declared that New York was not Dodge City.

Sitting there, as Media Person does, in his apartment, following the New York phantasmagoria day after day, it was all too easy to conclude that the city really had died and gone to hell.

There was a certain type of grotesque horror story that seemed typical of New York in the '80s and '90s.

An old woman is crossing the street in the heart of Manhattan. A car crashes into her, knocking her out of her shoes. It never stops. As the woman lies dying in the street, a man darts in and grabs her pocketbook and races off.

A mysterious bullet, perhaps fired from hundreds of yards away—no one ever finds out—hits a doctor sunning herself in Central Park on her lunch hour.

A thirteen-year-old boy kidnaps a ten-year-old boy on his way to school, ties him up and sets him on fire, almost killing him.

A gang of teenage girls roams the Upper West Side, jabbing pins into passing women at random, causing terror among the victims, who fear they might have been infected with AIDS needles.

A ten-year-old is found in school with a loaded gun in his pocket.

Deadly chunks of masonry rain down on unsuspecting pedestrians from eighteen floors up.

An ancient subterranean steam pipe ruptures, blasting a building with scalding steam and mud. When traces of asbestos are found, residents of the building are ordered out of their apartments. Work crews, dressed in special protective clothing, are sent in to clean up. The residents return to find their apartments looted and defaced, apparently by the workmen.

A young woman sitting in a restaurant with a friend is killed by bullets fired during an argument between drug dealers.

A gang of toughs call a Chinese restaurant and order takeout food. When the delivery man arrives, the crooks stab him and steal his bicycle.

For months, a man with a homemade blowgun roams midtown shooting tiny darts at women's buttocks.

A daily diet of such stories makes the New-York-Is-Dead patter seem plausible indeed.

But what does that mean, really? Media Person wondered: How could New York be dead if millions of people were still eating in its overpriced, noisy restaurants, getting raped in its subways, and enthusiastically stabbing each other on the flimsiest excuse?

Was it all mere bombastic media imagery? The media love colorful metaphors and catchy headlines like "NYC, RIP." Was it just a death-of-the-spirit kind of thing rather than a literal death? Media Person could live with that. Media Person's tough. After all, he's a New Yorker.

Was New York really dead? Media Person peered out the window through his binoculars. Cities can die, he knew. Babylon is dead. Machu Picchu is dead. Carthage is extremely defunct, and old Cortez pretty much put the kibosh on Tenochtitlán, a.k.a. the Big Taco.

But New York? Well, if you want to call the Wormy Apple critically ill, Media Person won't argue. If you swear New York is vomiting blood and has no pulse and a priest is administering last rites and an overly sincere Reform rabbi is preparing the eulogy . . . Okay, no problem.

But as long as one garbage truck is clanging and grinding wildly in the night and, somewhere in the South Bronx, a cop is returning a hallucinating psychopath's automatic fire, please—for Media Person's sake—don't write that New York is dead. Not yet. Save that finality for the day—it may come soon enough—that total silence descends on the smoldering, corpse-strewn rubble.

Because if the word gets out that New York is dead, maybe even the last few crazy holdouts will quietly tiptoe away. And Media Person will be left all alone in his dark building in this cold, empty ghost of a city, sitting there in front of his blank television screen, scared to death.

Myth America

As always, society today is beset by myths, shibboleths, and fables masquerading as truth. Too often the media unwittingly help spread these fallacies, an alarmingly high percentage of which involve TV weathermen. Over the years, Media Person has dedicated himself to rooting out the tedious falsehoods and replacing them with newer, more interesting lies of his own invention. This book is riddled with the latter. But here are just a few of the popular myths Media Person has exposed:

I. *Weathermen cause the weather.*

For many decades now, Media Person has been sending the following notice to all television news executives in the United States:

I can't stand it anymore. If you dimwits allow your anchorfolk once more to josh the weatherguy for bringing too much rain, I am going to burst into your studio with a high-caliber assault weapon and mow them all down like dogs. It is my firm belief that the bit is so lame *no jury in America will convict me.*

Of course, the TV executives just ignore Media Person and the anchors go right on doing it and never once does the weatherguy even say, "I didn't cause the rain, you little rodent; I just report it."

II. *The war on drugs is a great new idea and we will win it.*

It's not and we won't. We never win but we always forget we did all this before, and did it in the same phony way with politicians posturing and failing to attack root problems causing inner-city miseries. Sometimes drug use decreases for a while—until a new drug cycle and a new, popular drug come along. The public can't seem to remember much of anything, and the media's memory isn't much better so it whoops and cheers for the new war on drugs.

By now the score must be something like Drugs 5, Us 0. If this is a war, drugs have won.

III. *The great drought emergency is here again.*

Another memory loss. At some point in the winter, the TV weathermen in New York City grow alarmed about the water level. Standing dramatically in front of the reservoir upstate, trying bravely to keep the panic out of their voices, they reveal that a major calamity is coming: a drought. The water level is dangerously low and no relief is in sight. At this rate, the city will go dry. We will be helpless. We will all die a horrible death.

The politicians see this and start issuing dire warnings to alter our shower habits and place bricks in our toilet tanks and cut down on our drinking.

The citizens mostly ignore them. A few feel guilt and a vague anxiety but not enough to change their habits.

A few weeks later, it rains. End of drought. End of crisis.

Next time around no one remembers. The media fall for the hoax every time. No one checks the clips and sees that the same thing happened two years ago. No one checks the atlas and notes that New York ain't the Sahara, that dehydration has at no time been a leading cause of fatalities in the area.

IV. *TV weathermen serve some purpose.*

No they don't. They are totally unnecessary and the sooner society realizes it, the healthier we will be. In a sensible world, the

U.S. Weather Service forecast would be read by the anchor in approximately ten seconds, which is about all the weather info anyone wants.

That's why TV weathermen are always making trouble. They need to justify their worthless existences. They are dangerous people and should be watched. Or better yet, not watched.

V. *TV weathermen have to be either fat buffoons or good-looking, personable young people with professional haircuts and no personalities.*

Anyone could do it. *Anyone*. Milli Vanilli could do it.

VI. *Ginger Rogers did everything Fred Astaire did, only backwards and in high heels.*

Linda Ellerbee is believed to have originated the line. Ann Richards of Texas amplified it when she repeated it in her speech at the Democratic National Convention in 1988. It was a nice line, but it was wrong. Media Person explodes it only in the interest of truth and accuracy, certainly not to give solace to antifeminists.

Splendid as Ginger is, she really didn't do everything that Fred did, let alone backwards. For one thing, it was Fred who took the tricky solos; Ginger didn't dance on the ceilings or with hat racks. Also Fred did the choreography. And the heavy lifting.

Of course, whether Fred could have danced on the ceiling if he had to wear high heels is a question we'll probably never have answered.

VII. *Dan Quayle is a TV weatherman.*

Actually, he is vice president of the United States.

VIII. *I'm not middle-aged. Who lives to be 108?*

Whenever male writers do their inevitable mid–age crisis piece, they all come up with the same dumb line and they all seem delighted with their cleverness for having invented it.

Here's how Pete Hamill put it in *Esquire*: "That familiar phrase (middle age) is inaccurate; at 52, I am not in the middle of my life, for there is little chance that I will live to 104."

Johnny Carson did the same gag, though at least less windily. A guy of sixty-two calls himself middle-aged. "How many people do you know who are 124?" Carson cracked.

Well, how many people do you know who think that middle age

only lasts one year? Obviously, middle age is a period—a vague, imprecise period between youth and old age—and everyone recognizes it as such. So enough middle diddling.

IX. *Politics and sports are the same thing.*

The media love sports. They love sports so much that they try to turn everything else into sports. Wars have a way of quickly turning into sports events and politics even quicker.

This is because sports is easier to cover. In sports, there are only two sides and one wins and the other loses. The terms used to describe the events are simple, vivid, and colorful. Politics, on the other hand, can be dismayingly complex and difficult to explain. So why not turn it into sports?

USA Today once ran a disparaging story about how TV news campaign coverage shortchanges viewers on the issues and gives them mostly "horse-race stories." You know, who's ahead, who's raising the most money, and so on.

Meanwhile, on page 1 of the same paper was a story headlined:

POLL: BUSH, DUKAKIS ARE NECK 'N' NECK

Of course, to say that all newspapers and TV news shows turn politics into horse racing would be a gross oversimplification. The truth is that some of them prefer to turn politics into boxing.

A week of primary campaigning in the 1988 presidential election produced the following headlines in New York newspapers:

NEW YORK PUTS UP ITS DUKES!

KOCH, JACKSON TOE TO TOE AT THE BELL

THIRD-PLACE FINISH HAS GORE ON ROPES

DUKAKIS' BIG SPLASH MAKES HIM FAVORITE

Oh, yes, a passion for water polo occasionally sneaks in.

X. *You're our kinda people.*

Media Person isn't sure whether this is a myth or merely a delusion, but he doesn't have a chapter on delusions—so let's not stand on ceremony.

Besides, it's typical of a kind of annoying false logic you get from the media constantly.

It came to Media Person in a subscription appeal from *Utne Reader*, a kind of lefty *Reader's Digest* for people under eighty-five.

Dear Reader:

Are you socially hip? Or unhip?

Find out with this six-second test adapted from a story in the *San Francisco Chronicle*:

If you're unhip, claims the *Chronicle*, you shop in chain stores, buy disposable diapers, breakfast on glazed donuts, dine on formula-fed veal, have a housemaid named Maria, and wear a self-satisfied expression.

But if you're hip, you shop in mom-and-pop stores, buy cloth diapers, breakfast on oat-bran muffins, dine on free-range chicken, have a housemaid named Bob, and wear a worried expression . . .

. . . and what magazine do you read? According to the *Chronicle*, the unhip go for *People*. But if you're hip, you take UTNE READER.

Well, where does this leave Media Person? He doesn't read *People* or *Utne Reader* regularly, but occasionally looks at both. He has no maid named Bob or Maria. He buys no diapers at all. He breakfasts on neither glazed doughnuts nor oat-bran muffins. He eats chicken and veal but doesn't inquire into the origins of either. His customary expression is one of boredom, occasionally giving way to stark terror.

In other words he resists and resents pigeonholing and suspects that lots of other people do, too. The media love it, though, and so do the marketing boys.

You know, there are two kinds of people: those who let themselves be falsely classified by phony media definitions and those who don't.

Or is that a phony media definition?

XI. *The amazing prodigy.*

Every couple of years the newspapers get excited about some twelve-year-old Hungarian chess genius who is mowing down the opposition and will be the next Bobby Fischer. World's championship, here he comes.

Then you never hear of him again.

The papers never seem to notice that chess prodigies are a commonplace and few of them become world's champion.

XII. *A bad attitude can make you sick.*

This ridiculous story has become quite popular in the media over the past few years. The claim is that cheerful, optimistic people are healthier than depressed pessimists, who get sick more and die younger.

If this were true, Media Person would have expired *decades* ago.

He never would have made it past adolescence.

XII. *Some people see the glass as half full and others as half empty.*

The way Media Person sees it, the glass will soon be completely empty.

Hook You Now, Manipulator

Most media people are decent, law-abiding folk just like you and Media Person. But as in every occupational group, there are always the slick operators who rely on shortcuts, cute tricks, and sly moves to advance themselves. Through such antics, they can make slight stories look important, put careers on a faster track, increase circulation, bring down the government, or, at the very least, fill the news hole and get home quicker to a tasty dinner and a nice nap.

Media Person will now let you in on a few shady techniques. (He'd let you in on a lot but he wants to knock off early, too.)

QUOTE HOGS ON PARADE

You ever wonder why certain experts on TV start looking familiar? Because you see them all the time, is why.

Every newsroom in America has a Rolodex filled with names of talking heads on call. These are the instant experts, professional spouters of opinion, sound biters, and quote hogs. Aggressive, well-connected, media-wise yakkers mostly from Washington and New York, they love publicity and have learned to give short, punchy, colorful—yet predictable—answers to any question.

An arms-negotiation story is breaking? Every media outlet runs to call the same six experts, who are in everyone's Rolodex under ARMS. For the next few days, the big six are all over the tubes and the papers.

Any time a mass murderer is noticed by the press, the same shrink turns up with his perceptive analysis of the unknown killer: a loner with few friends who is hostile to women—if women have been his targets so far—or young black boys, or left-handed Albanian tinsmiths.

This system does not exactly make for great diversity of opinion or profound analyses of current events. It does, however, make for more exposure to the face of Henry Kissinger than is good for civilization.

SCRAWL TOGETHER NOW

To take notes or to tape quotes? That is the perennial question for print reporters. Taping a source is much more accurate—unless your tape recorder malfunctions and then you come back with a long hum. The problem is it takes time to play back interviews and transcribe them—often too much time for reporters working for dailies.

So most reporters do what reporters have done for aeons—scribble. They seldom learn formal shorthand; in the entire history of American journalism, only about six reporters have ever learned shorthand. No one knows why this is. Probably some great newsroom icon such as Greeley or Mencken or John Cameron Swayze proclaimed that shorthand was for sissies and no one has dared go up against them yet, not even Today's New Woman.

So every reporter develops his or her ingenious, homegrown method of speed scribbling, many of which are amazingly ineffective. One veteran newsman confided to Media Person:

"I can't read my own handwriting, so I get back to the office and make the quotes up. No source has ever challenged me yet and if one ever does, I'll just show him my notebook and say, 'Look, you said it; I've got it right here.' And he can't deny it because he won't be able to read it either."

WAR ALLEGEDLY HELL, SOURCES CLAIM

Wars are hard to cover. They're noisy, confusing, and can get you killed. But newspapers and TV love them because they're highly entertaining to everyone not actually in the path of the ordnance.

Lately the coverage of war has been greatly refined with the invention of the National Media Pool. Though the government thought it up, the media, for the most part, cheerfully went along. The concept worked brilliantly during the invasion of Panama. Rather than let large, unruly herds of media roam the battlefield, learning embarrassing truths, the Pentagon allowed fourteen reporters and cameramen to represent everyone. These were flown to Panama and locked in a room where they were treated to lectures from U.S. officials and permitted to watch television accounts from Cable News Network, which was reporting on the war from Atlanta.

The coverage of the war was excellent—by government standards. The media cheered the operation on, quickly pronouncing it a success, downplaying casualties, destruction, and incompetence, and raising few impertinent questions such as why four times more Panamanian civilians were killed than Panamanian soldiers. Once the happy little war ended, the media immediately returned to its habit of ignoring Panama. Since one of the justifications for the invasion had been that America was bringing democracy to the benighted nation, you'd think the media would be interested to check back now and then to see if we had succeeded. Nope. Panama sank back into poverty and despair amid a vast silence from the North.

HOLING THE FILLS

One of journalism's most closely guarded secrets is the amazing TK System of research, utilized by reporters at many leading newspapers and magazines.

A reporter knocking out a story but lacking a fact or two can fill the holes merely by typing "TK."

TK is journalese for "to come."

Say the reporter is exposing some political chicanery and wishes to compare it with previous scandals. Unfortunately, he can't recall the details of the old case. So he writes:

No sum this large has been stolen from a municipal government since 18TK when Mayor TK and his cronies looted $TK from the city treasury. He later served TK years in jail and died a broken man in 19TK.

It is now the job of someone else—a copy editor or fact checker or researcher or computer repairman—to dredge up and insert the info. When the article appears in print, all the TKs have been magically replaced by actual facts and the writer looks exceptionally well informed.

In writing this book, Media Person has utilized the TK System extensively. He has dealt in basic concepts and relied on others for the details. Media Person has full faith in the publishing industry and its vast resources and efficiency.

Media Person Answers the Big Questions

Those of you who have faithfully read this far will now be rewarded for your attention. Media Person will answer some questions of great import that are put to him frequently:

The meaning of life is TK.

What really happened to Amelia Earhart and Jimmy Hoffa was
TK.

John F. Kennedy was really killed by TK.

The answer, finally, to the question of whether there is a God,
whether there is life after death, whether there is any end to the
universe, and whether there is life on other planets is:

TK.

Invasion of
the Scribbling
Gawkers

Media Person was upset.

He'd gone out for the papers (about the only time he does go out) and the newspaper-magazine store was *on fire*.

It was full of firemen with hoses and the lights were out and Media Person could smell smoke. Rudy, the owner, was standing behind the counter in the dark, looking glum.

"Excuse me," said Media Person. "Are you open for business or should I be running for my life?"

No one thought this was funny. It's odd how people lose their sense of humor when they are on fire. Of course Rudy himself was not on fire but, for all Media Person knew, he could burst into flame at any second.

Media Person gathered what media he could (a couple of smoldering newspapers) and trudged home in despair, trailing wisps of smoke.

What a terrible year this has been, Media Person thought. And it was only January.

Things would get worse.

A few months later, Media Person was sitting calmly on his couch reading the papers when from someplace too nearby came a terrifying crash.

Trembling with fear, Media Person peeked out the window and saw an unlikely scene. An armored truck had careened across an intersection, climbed the sidewalk, and totaled an old, inoperative fire hydrant, a parking sign, and a mailbox. A mailbox into which, only an hour before, Media Person had placed a vitally important envelope that could change the course of his life!

He rushed outside to stand guard over the downed mailbox.

Not till postal rescue arrived and surgically extricated the mail did he dare leave his post, assured that he was safely back on track to win ten million dollars in the Publishers Clearing House Sweepstakes.

Amazingly, the removal of the armored truck took much longer and, when it happened, the towtruck managed to block the entire street, causing gridlock and a classic New York Screaming Idiots Festival when a berserk cabbie, unable to wait another second, tried to ooze his taxi between the tow-er and tow-ee.

But all this was nothing. A week later, Media Person's supermarket exploded.

The horror was indescribable. Media Person's own dear little supplier of pesticide-laden fruit, pollution-contaminated shellfish, and artery-clogging meat products was no longer content to decimate its customers gradually but now was trying to blow them up, putting the blame on some sort of gas problem, which was ironic as the food there often caused in Media Person the same condition.

This was the worst ordeal yet.

It brought *reporters* to the neighborhood. The last thing you ever want is a crazed pack of reporters loose in your neighborhood because the chances are they will be describing—with inordinate excitement—a thrilling disaster offering readers the promise of hair-raising death and destruction.

Yours.

Besides, reporters are deceitful scum who betray everybody they meet. Media Person knows this because he read it in the prestigious and respected magazine *The New Yorker* in an article by Janet Malcolm.

It was a rotten thing for Janet Malcolm to say and the fact that she was right was no excuse because now, Media Person feared upon reading her piece, no one with any sense would ever talk to a reporter again and then there would be no media and Media Person would have to spend his time knitting potholders.

Malcolm had dared to disclose a common journalistic technique that most reporters have used at one time or another but never admit, repressing the guilt so they may continue to function normally and not have to flagellate themselves in the company cafeteria.

She nabbed Joe McGinniss doing the deed in his best-selling true-life crime story, *Fatal Vision*. The trick is to suck up to a source, convince him you're his pal, string him along, get him to spill all while you sit there nodding and smiling ever so sympathetically.

And then you stick it to him.

This is Standard Operating Practice and necessary for the greater good of attaining a higher truth, or so expert witnesses William F. Buckley, Jr., and Joseph Wambaugh said when they testified on behalf of McGinniss, who was being sued at the time by Jeffrey MacDonald, McGinniss's subject, collaborator, and victim in *Fatal Vision*.

It's also, though this they didn't mention, a betrayal of trust, a form of lying, and more than a little creepy.

But is it wrong? Well, five of six jurors sided with MacDonald. They felt that McGinniss, the respectable famous author (and a good writer, too) had wronged MacDonald, *the convicted wife and child killer*.

Of course, most reporters don't carry their little seductions as far as McGinniss, who at one point had said in a letter to MacDonald:

Jeff, it's all so fucking awful I can't believe it yet—the sight of the jury coming in—of the jury polling—of you standing—saying those few words—being led out—and then seeing you in a fucking prison. It's a hell of a thing—spend the summer making a new friend and then the bastards come along and lock him up. But not for long, Jeffrey—not for long.

And of course Malcolm went too far in her much-quoted lead, which seemed to consign to hell all reporters who ever lived:

Every journalist who is not too stupid or full of himself to notice what is going on knows that what he does is morally indefensible. He is a kind of confidence man, preying on people's vanity, ignorance, or loneliness, gaining their trust and betraying them without remorse . . .

But this bit of overkill does not excuse the media hysteria that followed, the vituperation from outraged, self-righteous journalists who found more interest in attacking Malcolm ad hominem than discussing the issue she raised. Reading her fascinating analysis of the psychology of the journalistic interview, any honest reporter had to cringe at least a little.

Certainly a modicum of self-examination seemed in order. But like all humans, media types hate being criticized and prefer howling in rage.

After much rumination, Media Person decided that the solution to the problem is to force reporters, like police, to read sources their rights. This declaration would be called the McGinniss Warning and would have to be recited to all interviewees before commencing a Q & A.

It would go something like this:

You have the right to remain silent. You have the right to make one phone call to your PR consultant or media adviser. You have the right to say "no comment" or "this is off the record" or "I'll only talk to Barbara Walters and then only for big bucks." You have the right to know that even though tears are coming into my eyes, I don't necessarily believe one thing you tell me and in fact I'm planning to call your worst enemy who'll contradict everything you say and make you look like the biggest slime in the world right out in public where everyone can see it.

Now for my first question . . .

The Game of
the Name

Damn! It's not fair. Media Person figured out the '90s before anyone. Really, he did. He's got this decade pegged, but the only trouble is he can't come up with a catchy name like the Me Decade or the Roaring Twenties, so no one will pay any attention to him.

This means that once again Media Person will fail by a hair to become rich and famous. Whoever names the decade can live on it for, well, decades. Just Media Person's luck that he's stuck on a planet where style is valued over substance.

Naming a decade starts long before the decade does. Pundits had been trying to name the '90s as far back as the '80s but no one got it right. The consensus was the '90s would be all about noble public service and commitment to causes. We should be so lucky. The correct answer emerged in February 1990. It was then that Media Person realized that nothing was happening that was supposed to happen and everything was happening that wasn't. The news had spun totally out of control. This trend actually started in the '80s and was now accelerating.

The ratings were dropping for TV news broadcasts. People were tuning out the news. Why? Media Person realized it was because so much of it was *new* news.

That makes people nervous. What people like is old news. News they've been fed many times before and know how to digest and don't have to think about. People hate to think. It's tiring.

Communism is the enemy, that's the sort of thing people want to hear. Massacres in El Salvador, hurricanes in Florida, the war against drugs, the Arabs vs. the Israelis, incumbent congressmen being reelected. This is soothing news people can cope with. They already have their opinion on it and don't need to work up a new one.

But this new news. This '90s stuff. It scares the daylights out of us. For starters, it was ruining one of our few remaining certainties, that the commies were the bad guys and would never change.

Well, now the Russian Army voluntarily got out of Afghanistan, a McDonald's opened in Moscow, new governments formed in Czechoslovakia, Hungary, Poland, Romania, and Bulgaria, the Berlin Wall came down and East Germany went over to the other side, communism was collapsing all over Eastern Europe, the Cold War was over, NATO and the Warsaw Pact were obsolete, and Europe was trying to reshape itself into one big happy country.

All this happened in about two seconds.

Terrifying.

Not only that but South Africa was moving to end apartheid and released Nelson Mandela from prison. Canada seemed on the verge of dissolution. The United States had become a debtor nation. Mike Tyson, who everyone knew was the heavyweight champion of the '90s, was knocked out by some guy whose name no one could remember.

One week there was a massacre in Montreal, one of those crazed gunman things, and afterward people were saying, "We didn't think it could happen here. New York or L.A., sure, all the time, but not here."

They didn't get it. They hadn't caught on.

In the new news universe of the '90s, *anything could happen anywhere*.

All bets were off.

Then came the most awful new news of all. *7 Days*, the magazine that spawned Media Person, folded,* sending Media Person hurtling into a black void of nonexistence, his exquisite voice stilled except in a few precious copies of this book in the hands of rare individuals of high intelligence like you.

The '90s, Media Person knew, were the Breakaway Decade (an okay name but not a great name) in which no rule or assumption was safe. The only thing that could be predicted was that by the time the '90s ended, we would recognize nothing around us. The world was heaving itself into some completely new, as yet unknowable, but probably horrifying shape. Everything familiar and comforting would be swept away, replaced by a weird new landscape full of shaggy, menacing things that would keep us up worrying all night and probably eat us in the morning.

Even Media Person's favorite pastime, drinking tea with lots of honey, was threatened.

TINY BEE MITES DESTROYING
NATION'S HONEY INDUSTRY

he read in the paper, with a rising sense of hysteria.

This was it. The end was nigh. First New York, now the world.

What to do? How to survive the Breakaway '90s? Media Person has no idea. He can't even think up a name for them. Sorry, but you're on your own. Media Person has run out of advice and calm. He has rolled off his couch and lies quivering in a wretched heap on the floor, awaiting the worst.

The end of civilization as we know it is turning out to be really annoying.

*Remember the great magazine crash that Media Person predicted back on page 57? Little did he realize it would crash on top of *him*.

ABOUT THE AUTHOR

LEWIS GROSSBERGER was born in Brooklyn in
1941. After that, the documentation grows
sparse and the truth elusive . . . and when
you get right down to it, who cares?